Partnerships in Learning

Teaching ESL to Adults

JULIA ROBINSON
MARY SELMAN

Pippin Publishing

Acknowledgments

We would like to acknowledge the assistance of many people in preparing this book. We are grateful to the students who let us "learn on them" in our early and later days of teaching, to the professors who taught us, to students in teacher preparation programs, and to our colleagues. We would also like to thank the colleagues and friends who took time to give us very useful feedback—Tracey Derwing, Ann Hinkle, Anna Knowlson, Sumiko Nishizawa, Myra Thorkelson and Avril Tudeau-Bai. In addition, we would like to express our appreciation to Deborah Binnie Smith, Julia's colleague at Douglas College. She and Julia developed the Cross-Country Travel unit used as an example. We thank Jonathan Lovat Dickson for his encouragement to write the book and see it through to fruition. We also appreciate the support and enthusiasm of our families. We dedicate this book to them.

Copyright © 1996 by Pippin Publishing Corporation
481 University Avenue
Toronto, Ontario
M5G 2E9

Designed by John Zehethofer
Edited by Dyanne Rivers
Printed and bound in Canada by Friesens

Canadian Cataloguing in Publication Data

Robinson, Julia
        Partnerships in learning : teaching ESL to adults

(The Pippin teacher's library ; 23)
Includes bibliographical references.
ISBN 0-88751-074-4

1. English language - Study and teaching as a second language.* 2. Adult education. I. Selman, Mary. II. Title. III. Series.

PE1128.A2R62 1996   428'.0071'5   C96-930133-2

ISBN 0-88751-074-4

10   9   8   7   6   5   4   3   2   1

CONTENTS

Introduction 5

Learning a Second Language 7

Characteristics of Adult Learners 8
What Is Language? 11
Teaching and Learning Language 16
Approaches to Language Learning 18
Conclusion 21

Assessing Needs and Negotiating Curriculum 22

Assessing Needs 23
Analyzing Data and Negotiating Curriculum 33
Using Existing Resources 35
Conclusion 36

Planning Units 37

What Is a Unit? 37
Approaches 38
Why Organize by Units? 38
Planning Units 40
A Process for Unit-Planning 46
What Should a Unit Include? 52
Conclusion 55

Developing Tasks 56

Real-World Tasks and Enabling Tasks 57
Choosing Tasks 58
Kinds of Tasks 59
Choosing Resources 73
Conclusion 74

Planning Lessons 75

Elements of a Typical Lesson 75
Tasks: The Heart of the Lesson 80
Creating Lesson Plans 84
Conclusion 96

Putting Plans into Action 97

Managing the Classroom 97
Communicating with Students 108
Dealing with Problems 114
Encouraging Students to Learn outside the Classroom 117
Conclusion 119

Becoming a Dynamic Teacher 120

Developing Professionally 120
Functioning in an Institutional Context 124
Functioning outside the Institution 125
Conclusion 126

Additional Reading 127

. . . .

INTRODUCTION

Over the years, experienced practitioners have developed and refined a variety of approaches to teaching English as a second language to adults. *Partnerships in Learning* introduces the approach we use in our own teaching practice. This has evolved as a result of a variety of influences—our formal training for teaching both ESL and adult education, our own teaching experiences, and the expertise of helpful colleagues who have willingly shared their stories, ideas and philosophies with us.

Certainly, this book does not tell the whole ESL story, nor does it offer pat formulas. Rather, it provides an entry into the fascinating world of ESL teaching that we hope will inspire others to become knowledgeable about the basics and explore a variety of strategies and approaches.

Our approach integrates two fundamental understandings. The first is our understanding of how people most easily learn a second language. The second is our understanding of the principles of adult learning.

These understandings form the foundation of our beliefs about teaching ESL to adults:

— Collaboration between adult students and the teacher about content and process fosters effective learning.
— People most easily learn to use language when taught in a context that relates to their life experience, their existing knowledge and skills, and their goals.

— While language use is central to language-learning, focusing on specific skills improves the efficiency of the learning process.
— Language teachers benefit from the partnerships we form with students, fellow teachers and others in our institutions and communities.
— For students and teachers, learning is a lifelong process.

These beliefs pervade this book and helped us develop its structure. The first chapter introduces the learners and language, providing a brief historical perspective on language-teaching. The second discusses various methods of assessing students' needs and negotiating curriculum. This is followed in the next chapter by suggestions for developing units based on this assessment, as well as on the continuing assessment of needs that is critical to any program. The fourth chapter describes tasks and activities that facilitate learning, while the next suggests ways of preparing lessons in the context of the students' goals. The sixth chapter provides practical ideas for implementing lesson plans, and the book concludes with suggestions that have helped us continue to develop as teachers. For those who wish to delve more deeply into the ideas presented, a bibliography suggests additional readings.

Throughout, we recommend forming many kinds of partnerships—with students, colleagues and the community. These partnerships make teaching really satisfying and increase learning. In fact, in writing this book, our own partnership was a source of great pleasure and growth. It enabled us to integrate our experiences, beliefs and perspectives, sparking ideas that helped us develop fresh insights and support each other in the solitary task of "putting pen to paper." The fact that we are mother and daughter meant that these benefits were especially important.

Although we speak together, we have maintained our own voices. When we recount personal experiences, the voice is identified. We did not try to eradicate the distinction between our voices, and we feel the book is richer as a result.

Finally, we want to express our appreciation for the comments received from others when the material was in its final stages of development. These came from student teachers, beginning teachers, master teachers and teacher educators, as well as our editor, and helped strengthen the book.

. . . .

LEARNING

A SECOND LANGUAGE

Because our understanding of the students affects the way we teach, it makes sense to begin by focusing on who adult ESL learners are. Who are the people arriving in our classrooms—and why are they there? In addition, teachers need a fundamental understanding of language: what it is and why it's used. These understandings help us thoughtfully examine current approaches to teaching an additional language to adults and make informed decisions about both the learning and the teaching that goes on in our classrooms.

By describing our own beliefs about adult learners, language and language-learning, this chapter lays the foundation for the practical discussion of teaching and learning that follows. Fundamental to our philosophy is the belief that effective teaching is learner-centered, based on who the learners are—their language and psychological needs, as well as their goals. This approach values learners' experience and knowledge, their current language, culture and skills and ensures that they experience success.

As teachers, we must constantly examine and re-examine our beliefs about adult learners, language and language-learning to ensure that the choices we make in our teaching practice correspond to the philosophy that underpins our ways of doing things. We hope this chapter provides you with the tools needed to develop and expand your own philosophy and beliefs and explore techniques and strategies that are consistent with them.

Characteristics of Adult Learners

No matter what their background, adult learners often share certain characteristics that affect the process of learning another language and set them apart from younger ESL students. For example, unlike those of children, the first language skills of most adult students are likely to be fully developed when they arrive in our classrooms. Furthermore, adults have amassed a wealth of experience simply because they have lived longer than children. They come equipped with maturity, knowledge and cognitive skills. In addition, they often have adult responsibilities for working and caring for families. As a result, the time and energy they can devote to formal study may be limited. This means that they need to use the time they do have efficiently.

When people move to a new country or region, they may find themselves ill-equipped to handle a million everyday tasks simply because they don't speak the language. Tasks that were previously taken for granted, such as taking the bus, making a phone call or coping with shopping, can suddenly become obstacles. Furthermore, immigrants may face many other personal challenges: lack of a job; inability to land a job equal in status to the one held in their country of origin; lack of the personal support systems provided by family and friends; and responsibility for an extended family.

The need to carry out familiar tasks in an unfamiliar cultural environment can magnify the difficulties experienced by immigrants. When simple tasks suddenly become difficult or impossible because their language skills are limited or they are unfamiliar with the culture, their self-confidence and self-esteem can be weakened.

CULTURE AND ADULT LANGUAGE-LEARNING

Because culture is bound up with language, a variety of cultural factors can affect what happens in the classroom. For example, when ESL students first arrive, their concept of appropriate language, whether this involves level of formality or content, may be very different from that of the instructor.

Level of formality refers to the language style we use in particular situations; an employee speaking to the company president, for example, is likely to speak more formally and carefully than she would when talking to a friend. This style recognizes the social distance between the speakers. An example of inappropriate content might occur when students ask instructors their age. What is normal and supported in one culture may be an affront in another.

Furthermore, students may present their ideas in a less linear manner than the instructor is used to, and may be less concrete in their style of communicating. Attitudes that are perfectly natural in their home country may be at odds with those prevalent in their new culture. And, of course, the concept of appropriate behavior for men and women often varies widely from culture to culture.

In the classroom, ESL students may be used to responding quite differently to a teacher. For example, in some cultures, teachers have an elevated status as authority figures and the holders of knowledge. When the teacher asks a question, students customarily stand to respond.

Interactions between people, too, are often handled differently. For example, gratitude may be expressed non-verbally, or using people's names may not be as important as it is in Western societies. And, in some cultures, people express themselves indirectly; for example, rather than saying "no" directly, a speaker may use what seems to be a lengthy circumlocution.

The way people describe the world and fit things into categories also varies. For example, in Greek, one word describes the total appendage called the arm and the hand in English. Furthermore, some languages do not differentiate colors in the same way as English.

The difficulties inherent in learning a new language and settling into a new country can be magnified by cultural differences that adult learners do not comprehend. ESL teachers need to understand the roots of attitudes and various ways of seeing the world and help students adjust. As a result, it's important to devote class time to discussing cultural differences in an atmosphere of mutual respect.

INDIVIDUAL DIFFERENCES

Although adult ESL students often share certain characteristics, each is an individual and, as a result, even those from similar cultural backgrounds may be very different from one another. Their experiences, current circumstances, personal characteristics and competencies may vary widely.

Variations in students' socio-economic backgrounds, language, culture, work histories and exposure to formal education mean that their individual life experiences are often very different, a factor that can affect their performance in the classroom. If learners have had little or no formal education, for example, they may lack the self-confidence to participate actively in classroom activities and will probably need to acquire basic learning skills. If they lack literacy skills, they may be unable to access resources or note vocabulary or other information for study at home. And they may need an introduction to the kinds of classroom procedures that are taken for granted by those who have attended school.

Students who speak European languages are likely find learning English easier than those who speak languages that have little in common with English. For example, the grammatical structures, sound and writing systems of many Asian languages are very different from those of English. Furthermore, learners from very different cultural backgrounds need time and opportunity to gain insights into Western customs, attitudes and assumptions.

Those with work experience may possess education, training and skills that will help them learn. They may be motivated by the prospect of landing jobs once they become more proficient speakers of English. Others may be unemployed or seeking further education and training in preparation for entering the job market. Those with no history of work may look forward to training for a job as well as learning English. On the other hand, students who haven't worked and don't plan to are unlikely to be interested in work-related themes.

Students' current circumstances may involve their legal status as immigrants or citizens as well as their family situations. For example, the legal situation of some students may be under review, as in the case of refugees who are seeking asylum. The degree of stability of their status can affect their performance in the classroom.

Furthermore, students who are refugees or the spouses, parents or adult children of immigrants may not have chosen to leave their home country—or attend language classes. This can have a dramatic impact on their motivation to learn. For example, a man once arrived at one of our courses with his wife in tow. He pushed her forward and simply said, "Teach her!" Cases like this present very real challenges to teachers who need to find ways of motivating students.

Finally, students with heavy family responsibilities may have difficulty attending class regularly or studying outside class.

Students' personal characteristics involve their physical and emotional well-being, as well as their language-learning ability, styles and strategies. For example, some adults may be print-oriented learners who are most comfortable writing things down while others may be aural learners. In addition, the ages of the adult ESL students in a class may vary widely, a factor that can affect not only their priorities and interests but also the speed at which they learn.

Students' competencies are affected by their exposure to English and formal language-learning opportunities as well as their aptitude for language-learning. Furthermore, individual students may be strong in one language skill and weak in another. It's worth keeping in mind that all students have developed competencies as a result of their work, life experiences and interests; it's the teacher's job to draw on these.

When choosing and pacing classroom activities, teachers need to be aware of and take into account the individual differences among students. The next chapter offers specific suggestions for gathering and recording the kind of information needed to do this successfully.

What Is Language?

Language is a complex phenomenon that involves both meaning and form. Meaning is the content, while form is the combination of technical elements, such as grammar, vocabulary and pronunciation, that we use to say what we mean.

MEANING (CONTENT)

People learn language not to master its form but to communicate with others; in other words, learning a language is not an end in itself. This may seem self-evident, but how many of us, without the benefit of training in the field, might start by teaching the alphabet, which is devoid of meaning? Of course, students must learn the alphabet, but the emphasis needs to

11

be on learning the language necessary to interact effectively with others for communicative purposes.

The communicative purposes of language include getting things done, exchanging ideas, relating to others, and ensuring that our needs are met. For example, when talking to a potential employer, our communicative purpose may be to get information about job opportunities or to apply for a job.

People learn language most effectively when the communicative purpose is apparent. This is not to say that language learners don't need to master the grammar, vocabulary and sound system of English. They do. However, they learn most effectively when the technical aspects of the language are mastered in a context that has a clear communicative purpose relating to their experience, knowledge and needs.

This means that the focus of classroom activities needs to be on communication. When engaging in communicative activities, speakers, listeners, readers and writers create new meanings because of what they bring to the situation; namely, their knowledge, experience, frames of reference and expectations. No two people interpret what is said or written in exactly the same way. We make—and remake—our own meanings as we interact with others and react to and clarify input.

A communicative purpose involves one or more of the four language skills—the productive skills of speaking and writing and the receptive skills of reading and listening.

When we speak or write, for example, we usually do it to:

— Convey information (e.g., I'll be arriving on flight 262).
— Build and maintain relationships by conveying social messages (e.g., I hope you're feeling better).
— Express ideas and emotions (e.g., I miss you a lot).
— Ensure that our needs are met in various ways (e.g., I'd like two seats in the front).

When we read and listen, we usually do it to:

— Gather information (e.g., the TV schedule).
— Gather and explore ideas and points of view (e.g., the editorial page of a newspaper)
— Enjoy a story (e.g., reading fiction or true-life stories).
— Experience and gain insight into life experiences and emotions (e.g., stories and poetry).

When we communicate, we expect a result—and when the result is the one expected, it's very satisfying.

Mary: When I was in Indonesia, I learned how to ask a taxi driver to wait for me. The next time I got out of a taxi, I hesitantly put my new-found expertise to the test by saying, *"Tungo di sini."* Somewhat to my surprise, the driver nodded and waited. I was delighted to find that my linguistic effort had brought a tangible result—my request had been understood and acted upon. My success in this real situation helped me remember the phrase; it reinforced my learning.

This is an example of the real use of language and it's what we aim for in the classroom—to help students engage in tasks that require them to use real language to fulfill real intentions. By focusing on meaning that relates to their needs and concerns, we help learners become involved in and develop a personal commitment to learning. When they are able to communicate meaning, they not only provide the content or context for their own development as speakers of English but also learn the technical elements of the language needed to communicate clearly and precisely.

Adult ESL learners have already developed their own personal models of the world and are experienced at making meaning in their first languages. When they come to an ESL class, they bring these meanings with them. In the class, they need to learn not only to express these meanings in English, but also to invent new meanings as a result of the remarkable experience of being in a new culture and environment. By involving them in creating relevant ideas in English, we encourage them to be active, motivated learners.

FORM (COMBINATION OF TECHNICAL ELEMENTS)

When we read, write, speak and listen, we make meaning by integrating and applying a variety of linguistic and non-linguistic elements of language—grammar, language functions, vocabulary, the sound system, language skills (listening, speaking, reading and writing), body language and cultural insights.

Grammar: Because English is rule-governed to a point and students will be looking for these rules to serve as guideposts as they try to make sense of the language, ESL teachers must be familiar with the basics of English grammar.

While comprehensive grammar texts are useful references, texts designed specifically for ESL students make a good starting point for widening our knowledge of grammar and finding ways to give learners useful explanations. Betty Azar's *Fundamentals of English Grammar* is a particularly helpful guide.

Language functions: Language functions refer to what we do with language; for example, request, report, express regret and persuade. These functions can be expressed in a variety of ways, depending on the precise shade of meaning we wish to convey. For example, if we were trying to persuade someone to come to a meeting, we might say, "I hope you will come," "I want you to come," "It is important for you to come," "Please come," or "I really want you to be there."

Vocabulary: New words are introduced most effectively in a context that is familiar to the learners. When focusing on particular words, we need to help students develop strategies for understanding the relationships among words and decoding the meaning of words in context.

Sound system: The English sound system involves pronunciation, stress and intonation patterns. When teaching ESL, it's important to focus on sounds in English that do not occur in the students' home languages. For example, we might help them hear the difference between sounds they confuse (e.g. *s* and *th* as in "sink" and "think") and show them how to make sounds using speech organs such as the lips, teeth, nose, gum ridge and larynx.

Pronunciation Contrasts by D. and A. Nilsen is a useful reference, but do not attempt to teach pronunciation directly from it. Judy Gilbert's book, *Clear Speech: Pronunciation and Listening Comprehension in North American English*, is also a helpful guide.

When conveying meaning in English, stress and intonation are at least as important as pronunciation because they create the music or rhythm of the language. Using these elements of the sound system correctly is an important key to understanding and being understood.

Stress occurs on syllables within words and on key words in sentences. Stress in English is irregular and must be learned, especially by students who speak regularly stressed languages, such as French.

Intonation refers to the rising and falling patterns in speech and indicates the intent of an utterance. Applying a different intonation to the same words can alter the meaning dramatically (e.g., He likes beer. He likes beer?).

Stress patterns and the range of intonation vary among languages. For example, some Indian languages have little stress and a narrower intonation range than English. In English speech, we tend to link words by attaching the final consonant sound of one word to the initial vowel sound of the next (e.g., "He went out" becomes "He wen tout" in speech).

Language skills—*listening, speaking, reading and writing*: To be fluent and accurate, students must develop and practice these skills extensively in a variety of contexts.

The receptive skills of listening and reading require active attention, because the content and language forms are unpredictable. To listen and read efficiently, students must learn to use a variety of sub-skills, such as focusing on key words and using context clues.

Because speaking and writing are productive skills, the speaker or writer has more control over the content. Speaking and writing require us to create meaning by integrating our knowledge and skills.

Body language: Body language conveys meaning without using words. It includes gestures and facial expressions that are characteristic of, and integral to, each language and culture, and must be learned along with the language. For example, the unwritten rules of eye contact often differ among cultures.

Cultural insights: Because culture is closely tied to language, it is part of language-learning programs. It includes assumptions and expectations about attitudes and behavior and affects the content or meaning we choose and the way we express it. When discussing culture, it's important to establish respect for the cultures of others as the class norm.

When we teach English to <u>immigrant</u> students, we often find that they also need—and want—to learn a number of other things, including:

— How the culture of their new country works.
— How to access community resources.
— How to integrate into the society.
— The rights and responsibilities of citizens.
— What citizens should know about the country.

Teaching and Learning Language

HOW ADULTS LEARN ANOTHER LANGUAGE

Adult language learners have already shown that they are perfectly capable of learning a language. Our task is simply to help them learn another. The following chart compares the way babies learn their first language with the way adults learn an additional language.

Language-Learning: A Comparison

Learning first language as a baby	Learning an additional language as an adult
No time pressure	Pressure to learn to meet other goals (e.g., work or study)
No embarrassment	May be embarrassed by errors
Surrounded by language related to physical events	May lack opportunity to hear English they can understand
No pressure to speak	May be required to speak
Experiments with sounds; learns all English sounds	Expects to make meaningful sounds; must learn unfamiliar sounds; may confuse unfamiliar sounds (e.g., *d* and *t*)
Uses language to get basic needs met	Meets own basic needs—needs are more complex

Exposed to simple language about simple matters	Wants and needs to handle complex topics and abstract concepts
Parents tolerate and enjoy errors	May experience negative reactions to errors
Parents support language-learning	May lack support
Cries to compensate for lack of language needed to get needs met	May rely on dictionary or translator or be unable to communicate
Usually has acute hearing	Hearing may be less sharp, especially if older
Unable to analyze	Can analyze language patterns
Can use only oral language	If literate, can use reading and writing to support learning
Starts with single words	Starts with single words
Has no language to begin with	Has a first language that differs from English
No preconceived notions about how to learn language	May have preconceived notions about how to learn language

When thinking about how adults learn another language, it's helpful to reflect on our own language-learning experiences by asking ourselves the following questions:

— What language skills did I develop?
— Did I learn by memorizing, learning rules, writing exercises or engaging in interactive activities?
— How well did the atmosphere build my confidence in using the language?
— To what extent did I learn language that I could use?
— If the teacher now asked me to suggest ways of improving the classes, what would I say?

It may be useful to note the answers to these questions in the back of this book or in a personal journal. Because we tend to teach the way we were taught, reflecting on our own language-learning experiences helps us consider how we would like to adjust our teaching.

N.B.

Approaches to Language Learning

Over the years, approaches to teaching language have evolved dramatically. Although some once-popular approaches now seem passé, they made an important contribution to the field and, in many cases, some aspects are still useful. To show how the field has evolved, we'll briefly examine some of the language-teaching methods often mentioned in ESL literature. More extensive information is available in other books such as *Teaching English as a Second or Foreign Language*, edited by Marianne Celce-Murcia.

In the past, much language-learning was designed to teach people the grammar and vocabulary of the target language so they would be able to read it. This was natural, considering that some of the languages, such as Latin or Ancient Greek, were no longer spoken. Often referred to as the grammar-translation approach, this method emphasized learning grammar rules and translating text, a focus that carried over to the teaching of modern languages.

The drawback to the grammar-translation approach is, of course, that it leaves learners ill-equipped to use a language in everyday conversation. As people began to understand the importance of teaching a language so that it could actually be spoken, the emphasis began to shift. New teaching approaches were developed on the basis of notions of how people learn language. At one stage, the view was that learning a new language was simply a matter of habit formation and, as a result, mimicry and memorization became the dominant techniques.

Called the audio-lingual approach, this method emphasized correct form and was greatly influenced by behaviorist psychology and structural linguistics. To paraphrase Professor Higgins, it didn't matter *what* you said as long as you got the grammar right. The goal was to enable students to produce error-free language.

The cognitive-code approach, on the other hand, emphasized the mental capabilities of learners. It involved learning and applying the rules of grammar. As a result, many students learned the grammar but had trouble creating the language they needed to communicate.

Another development occurred when theorists began to recognize that people's emotional states affect their ability to learn; relaxed students learn more easily than those who are tense. Various strategies for increasing the comfort of learners were developed, from playing relaxing music to encouraging students to sit in armchairs (suggestopedia) and using the learners' first language in a free-flow conversation while English equivalents were provided by bilingual teacher aides (counseling-learning).

The connection between language and the situations in which it is used is paramount in what is called the situational approach, while meaning and the cultural appropriateness of language in specific contexts is of great importance in communicative language teaching. Both these approaches focus on communicating meaning in real or realistic contexts.

The total physical response method is based on the way babies learn and holds that language is closely related to body movement. Its proponents recognize the value of involving learners in activities such as playing games, participating in hobbies or following and giving directions that call for active physical responses.

The functional-notional approach emphasizes the functions of language and the various forms that can be used to fulfill functions such as apologizing, making requests and giving compliments. The choice of form depends on the situation, the relationship between the speakers, and the level of formality called for. Notions refer to concepts such as time and space.

In this approach, the needs of the learners, their social context, and their culture became prominent. Learners' experience and knowledge were used as a framework for language development.

Proponents of the natural approach view language-learning as a holistic undertaking with the learner, rather than the language, at its center. It focuses on acquiring a language "naturally," through exposure to comprehensible input rather than through the systematic study of language forms.

Advocates of the task-based approach believe that learners must be involved in making meaning and negotiating meaning with others. They need to use language while carrying out tasks and attend to form in the context of making meaning.

Content-based instruction is associated with English for special purposes and academic study. Subject matter relevant to the needs of the student is used to teach language. A variety of models of content-based teaching have been developed.

Clearly, all these approaches have influenced the way ESL is taught today and echoes of all can be found throughout this book. Few, if any, teachers adopt one single approach and stick to it rigidly; rather, we tend to pick and choose, selecting elements of various approaches and tailoring them to the needs of the learners and our own philosophy, beliefs and teaching style.

For example, although the grammar-translation approach is not in vogue, many teachers recognize that simply translating a word is sometimes the quickest way to help a learner comprehend. Mimicry and memorization gave way to a recognition that intensive practice of a grammatical structure or vocabulary can take place in meaningful, interactive contexts, such as small groups. Working in groups has been shown to reduce stress and increase students' participation and opportunities to practice speaking the language. Furthermore, carrying out tasks often combines physical activity and language.

CURRENT APPROACHES

As today's teachers take the initiative to conduct their own research into teaching and learning a second language and work together to develop curriculum, teaching materials and techniques, it isn't unusual to find their approaches based on a combination of theoretical research and actual classroom experience. As previously indicated, many teachers use elements of various approaches to serve their purposes and the students' needs. The main shift has been in these directions:

— Communicative purposes are emphasized.
— The personal needs of the learners are the basis for selecting both content and process.
— Students learn the language that is used in the community.

As this shift has occurred, the concept of the teacher's role has also changed:

— The teacher is a facilitator and a learning resource rather than an instructor.
— The teacher collaborates with students to select goals, content and processes for the classroom.
— The teacher encourages students to develop independent learning skills.

As a facilitator, the teacher's role is to work in partnership with the students to create situations and develop tasks that encourage them to take the initiative, and create and practice language. As students participate, they have many opportunities to develop and express their ideas (make meaning). Facilitation does *not* mean that the teacher stops setting directions, proposing content or evaluating achievement. Decisions in these areas require the knowledge and skills of the professional. The goal is to interact with learners in a way that helps them make meaning. Specific strategies for achieving this goal are discussed in the chapters that follow.

Conclusion

The starting place for teaching language is the learners—who they are and what they need to learn in order to cope in an English-speaking environment so that they can achieve their personal goals. From this starting point, teachers work with the learners to make decisions about topics and activities that will help them progress toward their goals.

The starting place for language-learning is communicating meaning. People learn to use English effectively when they can associate it with actions and ideas that have meaning for them. The elements of language, such as grammar and vocabulary, are the essential tools that enable this communication to take place.

The various approaches to language-learning that have been popular over the years all have something to teach us. By using them selectively and assessing their merits in particular situations, we can benefit. However, no single approach suits all students in all situations.

Some of the ideas mentioned will be developed more extensively in the chapters that follow. In the next, we offer suggestions for assessing learners' needs and working with learners to negotiate curriculum, the first steps in the planning process.

. . . .

ASSESSING NEEDS AND

NEGOTIATING CURRICULUM

If we believe that effective teachers use a learner-centered approach, it's important to find out who the learners are. To do this, we conduct a needs assessment, a process that involves gathering information about students' abilities and goals, as well as their language and personal needs. This information is essential for negotiating curriculum and planning courses.

The needs assessment enables us to tailor the content as well as the process of a course to the needs, interests and abilities of specific learners. By addressing the particular needs of a specific group, we not only make the best use of students' time, which is probably at a premium, but also stimulate participation and learning. Furthermore, taking part in the needs assessment process encourages adult students to feel a degree of control over their destiny in the class.

The needs assessment is not completed in a day. It is a cyclical process that starts long before we meet the students and continues throughout the course. When we first meet students, a preliminary assessment helps us develop an initial sense of who they are. As the class meets and we get to know them, the needs assessments become more detailed, enabling us to flesh out the units of the course as it progresses and accommodate emerging needs. Some needs assessment activities are specific and involve the students. Others, such as the teacher's observations, are more subtle. However, all contribute to forming an overall picture of the students' common needs that helps us plan successful, learner-centered activities.

The process of assessing needs and negotiating curriculum involves three components—information exchange, assessment activities and negotiation. It's important to note, however, that these components are not discrete, nor do they follow one another in lock-step fashion; in fact, they are cyclical and tend to overlap.

The information exchange component involves teacher and learner in sharing personal information. It may include exchanging views about how to learn a language, assessing students' language competencies, and discovering both their expectations of the language class and personal background information. Critical to this is finding out about the students' goals. Do they intend to enroll in further education and, if so, what kind? Are they after certification in their field of work? Do they want to improve their ability to communicate with their children's teachers?

The assessment activities component involves specific strategies for identifying students' needs, goals, abilities and interests, while the negotiation component involves finding common goals and needs among the students that can help us work together to decide on themes and ways of learning, and set priorities for skills that need developing.

Assessing Needs

Needs assessment helps increase motivation and self-esteem by recognizing students' interests and abilities and valuing their own assessment of what they need to learn. Students who are learning material they have identified as important are more likely to be enthusiastic learners. In addition, by engaging them in the decision-making process, we send the message that we view them as colleagues and encourage them to take more responsibility for their own learning.

The assessment process also helps us find out what learners already know. Equipped with this information, we can acknowledge and build on the skills they already possess by linking new knowledge to what they already know. When the teacher values their skills and cares about their interests and goals, their confidence and self-esteem are enhanced.

Furthermore, when learners talk about themselves and negotiate goals, they are practicing English. Using language for this kind of real purpose helps increase their motivation and their learning.

The needs assessment process enables the teacher to establish goals in consultation with the learners and plan both the program and specific lessons. It also helps us focus on the learners' competencies and needs rather than on an arbitrary choice of an element of language.

Needs assessments of different kinds take place in three phases—before the first meeting of the class, during the initial meetings of the class, and on a continuing basis. Although assessing needs is a cyclical process, we tend to assess certain things at certain times, though this, of course, is flexible and open to endless modifications.

ASSESSING NEEDS BEFORE CLASSES BEGIN

Before the class meets for the first time, it's important to become familiar with the learners—and the issues that affect them. At this stage, we can gather two kinds of information: information about individual students and information about their community.

Student Information

Many institutions have introduced a system of interviewing, testing and placing learners before courses begin. This is a great advantage, especially if the teacher is part of the process, because it enables us to get to know individual students ahead of time and obtain important information about their backgrounds.

Furthermore, an institutional registration form can provide a focus for personal interviews that help us assess students' listening and speaking abilities. And, if students are required to complete an assessment test, this can provide information about their proficiency in English. Although tests such as this certainly give us a broad sense of their competence, it's worth noting that further assessment is needed to establish specific goals, needs, abilities and interests.

When institutions don't provide an opportunity to conduct this kind of pre-program assessment, it may be necessary to wait until the class meets to start gathering information about individuals.

Community Information

Teachers need to understand the community in terms of the specific issues and services that relate to the students. For example, we should be familiar with immigration patterns and socio-economic issues related to employment, housing, immigration and health. In addition, we need to be aware of community resources in the areas of health, welfare, recreation and education.

Information on issues such as these is often available from a variety of sources—other teaching staff and administrators, cultural agencies, newspapers, health departments, school counselors, government reports and public libraries.

ASSESSING NEEDS DURING INITIAL CLASSES

The needs assessment that takes place during the initial meetings of the class encourages learners to engage in the process and provides information that helps identify some of their goals. As we discuss these goals with them and negotiate which will be worked on, we begin making more detailed plans for the first topic or theme of the course.

At this stage, it helps to explain why we're interested in finding out about their needs and to invite them to participate in the process. Because this experience may be new to them, it's important to ensure that they understand what we're trying to do by talking about both the purpose and the expected outcomes of the exercise. While making it clear that we're knowledgeable about language-learning, we explain that we need to find out more about them and their level of proficiency in English in order to tailor a program that will help them learn. At this stage, interpreters—often available among students in advanced classes or through cultural agencies—may provide useful assistance.

It's a good idea to start an information file for each student and add to it as the course progresses. The following headings provide an outline of the kinds of information that might be included in the files. Be aware, however, that students may be reluctant to discuss some topics and be ready to back off; students have a right to privacy and to decide what information they wish to share. As they get to know us better, they usually become more willing to disclose personal information. Of course, it's the teacher's responsibility to maintain their trust by keeping all such information confidential.

— *Personal data*: Age, country of origin, length of time in the country, first language, other language(s), occupation in home country, occupation now, years of formal education, family responsibilities, interests.
— *Goals*: Educational, occupational and personal.
— *Themes*: Themes of interest to learner (e.g., work, citizenship), roles played in relation to theme (e.g., employer, employee), language contexts in which roles are played (e.g., office, factory), language uses (e.g., listening to instructions).
— *Language proficiency*: Interview findings, test results, observations of skills.
— *Learning*: Learning styles and preferences, learning strategies, previous education.
— *Community knowledge*: Knowledge of community resources and how to access them, cultural information (e.g., assumptions and expectations of the community).

Strategies

During the initial classes, one of our goals is to identify both how the students use language and how they would like to be able to use it. To do this, we need to find out:

— Themes that are important to them (e.g., family life, jobs or consumer tasks).
— The roles they now perform (e.g., parent, worker or homemaker).
— The contexts in which they perform these roles (e.g., as a parent communicating with health-care professionals, as a worker communicating with supervisors, etc.).
— Their current level of proficiency in English (e.g., how well they can perform tasks that require use of English).
— Their knowledge of the community, how to access its services, and how its culture compares with their own.

Identifying Themes

Because students who are just beginning to learn English may have trouble articulating the kind of information outlined in the previous section, it helps to provide them with visuals depicting locations such as stores, the doctor's office, a bank, restaurants, schools, workplaces and a recreation center. The visuals chosen depend on our knowledge of the students and their community. Invite them to choose the five locations where using English is most important. Tabulate their responses and present the top three or four as the ones of greatest interest to the class. Be sure to check that students are satisfied with the choices.

Alternatively, we can ask them to name places they frequently go, such as the drugstore, post office, bank or business office. With the group, make a list of these places and invite the students to identify three places on the list where they most need to use English.

Identifying Roles and Contexts

Once a theme of common interest is identified, the next step is to establish how the learners relate to it: the roles they perform and the context in which they perform them. For example, if a work theme is of interest, do students relate to it as job applicants, employees or in some other way?

Working with the group to create a web like the one illustrated is one strategy for finding contexts of common interest. For example, if the students have indicated that, as consumers, they have trouble dealing with the phone company, brainstorm to find out what they deal with now and what they want to be able to deal with in future. On the web, record an example of a context, such as getting a phone. Then brainstorm ideas for other contexts. They may come up with things like figuring out bills, moving to a new address, or making a complaint.

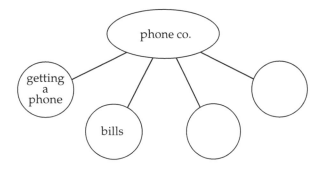

Identifying Tasks

To identify students' learning needs and develop related learning activities, the web can be extended by exploring in greater detail the tasks that must be performed in each context. For example, focusing on bills in the web illustrated may reveal that the learners have trouble reading their bills and dealing with errors when they find them.

The teacher then analyzes the tasks involved in resolving the problem and develops activities designed to assess students' needs. One way of doing this is to create a chart like the the following, which lists the tasks involved in questioning a telephone bill in the left column. The assessment activities students will be asked to perform are in the middle column and the skills needed to complete each are noted on the right.

The needs revealed by this process form the basis of planning for the unit. Although this example is very detailed, the process becomes easier as we get to know the students and deepen our awareness of their needs.

Dealing with Errors on a Telephone Bill

Tasks	Assessment Activities	Skills Demonstrated
Find key information	Circle specified information (e.g., amount due, balance)	Understanding bill format, scanning, reading words and phrases
Check accuracy of bill	Underline long-distance calls	Scanning, identifying long-distance calls
Telephone customer service	Locate number in directory, role-play conversation	Using appropriate language and content
Understand questions	Respond to requests for identifying information (e.g., name, phone no.)	Responding appropriately
Explain problem	Role-play in pairs	Explaining facts
Understand response	Listen to tape of brief explanations and summarize	Listening accurately, relaying information

Dealing with Errors on a Telephone Bill

Tasks	Assessment Activities	Skills Demonstrated
Accept or reject explanation	Role-play	Stating opinion appropriately
Understand options	Brainstorm possibilities	Dealing with bureaucracies and explaining possible outcomes
If explanation rejected, write a letter	Write letter of explanation	Writing business letter

Identifying Students' Strengths and Weaknesses

As the students carry out the assessment activities, we need to observe how well they perform in the following specific areas. This helps us evaluate not only their overall proficiency in English, but also specific factors that may affect their prospects of learning efficiently.

Language functions: Are they able to use the appropriate language for carrying out specific purposes? In the case of the error on the telephone bill, for example, these purposes include giving personal identifying information, explaining a problem, and accepting or rejecting an explanation.

Elements of language: How proficiently are they able to use specific elements of language, such as grammar, pronunciation, intonation, vocabulary and spelling?

Language skills and sub-skills: How strong are their language skills—listening, speaking, reading and writing—and pertinent sub-skills, such as scanning for information and listening to get the gist?

Learning styles: Adult students may be used to particular ways of learning as a result of their childhood educational experiences. We need to know what these are and take them into account.

Task types: How do they adapt to the various kinds of tasks involved in a specific activity? The phone bill activity, for example, includes role-playing, brainstorming, working in pairs and individual writing tasks.

Learning strategies: Can they ask for help? Do they use dictionaries and other resources, keep records of grammar corrections and new vocabulary for review, and use each other as resources?

Communication strategies: How do they currently meet their communication needs? For example, do they rely on family members to translate or perform tasks for them, use visual cues to help them understand, or focus on grammatical correctness rather than communicating?

The notes we make during this process help guide us when planning lessons, a topic that will be discussed in greater detail in the next chapter. Once a theme is completed, the needs assessment tasks can be used again to assess students' progress.

ASSESSING NEEDS AS THE COURSE UNFOLDS

As the course unfolds, we use and refine the data we already possess and gather more detailed information on the needs identified initially. As students feel more at ease with this process, they may mention additional needs themselves. And, as time passes and their skills improve, new needs may also emerge.

Sometimes teachers are so eager to start teaching that they're reluctant to spend much time on needs assessment. Bear in mind that needs assessment activities can provide language-learning opportunities and vice versa; engaging in language practice activities can reveal needs. For example, asking students to choose between two alternative goals, such as learning to tell time or learning to talk about money, helps them practice expressing preference (e.g., I'd like to learn to tell time in English).

While the initial focus of classroom activities is on needs assessment, the balance between assessing needs and engaging in actual language-learning activities begins to shift as the class continues to meet. Once the teacher develops a sense of the students' common and individual needs and goals, language-learning activities designed to meet these assume greater importance.

Assessing the students' needs is a continuous process for two reasons:

— To enable us to adapt the program to meet students' needs to learn specific skills that may arise during the course.
— To enable us to develop plans for subsequent units in greater detail.

Furthermore, the continuing assessment sometimes reveals that some of the educational or occupational goals initially identified by the students are not realistic. As part of the process, we need to help students consider their goals, often in terms of the time and effort that will be necessary to achieve them. To do this, it helps to invite advanced ESL students with similar language backgrounds and education to describe their experiences with language-learning.

Observing Students' Specific Needs

At this stage of the process, we rely primarily on our own observations to gather information about students' emerging needs. As the students work on activities, we constantly observe their styles, strategies, cultural knowledge and knowledge of how to access information, as well as the way they are able to use elements of language and the language skills.

Language skills: To assess proficiency in the language skills, it helps to think in terms of receptive skills—listening and reading—and productive skills—speaking and writing.

The receptive skills involve comprehending the spoken and written word. To do this, learners need to know grammar and vocabulary. They also need to be alert to discourse markers, such as "for example" and "first," that help guide them through a language experience, and to comprehend both explicit and implied meanings. When listening, they need to be able to discriminate between sounds and understand the implications of particular intonation and stress patterns.

The productive skills of speaking and writing also require a knowledge of grammar and vocabulary. Writing, of course, requires spelling skills. Speaking requires fluency or a smooth flow of language, as well as comprehensible pronunciation, stress and intonation.

Learning Strategies: While teachers must be aware of and respect the learning strategies used by students, we also need to help them develop alternative strategies. For example, some students rely exclusively on strategies developed during their earlier schooling experiences. These may include memorizing, reciting and using bilingual dictionaries.

Showing respect for these strategies by initially working with the students' preferences helps us gain their trust, ensuring that they will feel comfortable about trying new strategies at the appropriate time.

The following questions help guide our observations:

— Do the students use units of meaning—groups of words that represent an idea? Proficient readers comprehend meaning by reading in phrases rather than word by word. Proficient listeners listen to the flow and don't get caught up in puzzling over individual words.
— Do they take risks? Are they willing to try new language and comfortable about learning from their mistakes?
— Do they use context—the situation and the clues it provides to help make meaning? For example, when reading, do they use titles, pictures, charts and diagrams?
— Do they tolerate ambiguity? Are they willing to accept partial understanding of something they hear or read in the belief that the full meaning will eventually become apparent?
— Do they make use of redundancies? Are they alert to the built-in repetitions that help make meaning?
— Do they work around their limitations? Do they see alternative ways of expressing themselves?
— Do they ask others for help? Do they ask for meanings and for ways of expressing themselves? Do they listen carefully to other students' speech and use it as a model?
— Do they observe and imitate native language models?
— Do they look for opportunities to practice language?
— Do they ask for feedback and practice corrections?
— Do they emphasize communication or accuracy of language forms?

Observing these practices provides clues about how we can help students become effective learners. Specific suggestions for helping students develop effective strategies are included in the chapter titled "Putting Plans into Action."

Developing More Detail for the Next Unit

The initial needs assessment activities usually provide a general idea of the themes that will make up the units of study. As we near the completion of the first unit, however, we begin a more detailed needs assessment that helps us flesh out plans for the next unit.

Analyzing Data and Negotiating Curriculum

With the first few classes under our belts, it's time to analyze the assessment data we've collected and begin negotiating curriculum. The following strategies help us do this:

— Focus on the learners' common goals rather than on individual language proficiency. For example, some learners aspire to enter educational programs and some to re-enter the professions they practiced in their country of origin; others simply want to learn enough English to cope with specific situations such as work, shopping or banking.

— Look for common interests and concerns identified during the initial needs assessment. Developing a chart like the following helps identify commonalities.

Student	*Tony*	*Ming*	*Zarina*

Background
    Years of education
    Work			

Goals
    Educational
    Occupational
    Personal			

— Formulate some goals and negotiate these and the kinds of activities that will help achieve them. Naturally, the students will need to experience different kinds of learning activities before they are able to express their preferences.

— Formulate an overall plan based on the priorities identified by the students, our knowledge of language and our observations of the students. The following chapter deals with this element of the process in greater detail.

When negotiating the choice of themes that will make up the curriculum, it works well to divide the students into groups of three or four, inviting each group to come up with its own preferences. Beforehand, we copy four or five of the most popular topics onto sets of index cards. Each group receives a set of cards and, through discussion, settles on an order of preference. The groups then post their cards in order and explain their choices to the other groups.

These explanations usually reveal some of the contexts in which students want to be able to handle specific language tasks more effectively. For example, if "neighbors" is a topic, the students may say things like, "I want to get to know my neighbors," or "I want to explain something to my neighbors."

When a wide variety of needs and interests is revealed, compromise may be necessary. Students may need to choose themes that are not high priorities for everyone or the teacher may need to offer alternatives or suggest dealing with subjects of greater interest later in the course. Suggestions for individualizing the curriculum are offered in the chapter titled "Putting Plans into Action."

The process of negotiating curriculum is never without constraints, which may affect both the teacher and the learners. Being aware of these ahead of time helps everyone cope.

Constraints That May Affect Negotiation of Curriculum

Teachers	Learners
Institutional requirements	Ability to comment on needs
Teaching experience	Inexperience with assessment
Preferred teaching styles	Role expectations for teachers and learners
Time	Concept of selves as learners
Materials and resources	Ability to analyze selves
Diversity of needs and abilities within group	Diversity of needs and abilities within group

In summary, the process of conducting needs assessments, dealing with the data revealed, and negotiating curriculum consists of the following steps. The steps are not necessarily completed in this order, however. We often move back and forth among them.

Assessing Needs and Negotiating Curriculum—the Process

Gather data on students' backgrounds, goals, topics of interest, abilities and strengths and weaknesses

⇓

Analyze data to discover similarities and differences

⇓

Negotiate choice of themes and contexts with learners by establishing preferences

⇓

Outline overall plan—themes, contexts and skills to be worked on—and request feedback from students

⇓

As course progresses, modify plan and add detail through further needs assessment activities

Using Existing Resources

Why don't we simply leave the curriculum up to the experts or find a good textbook and follow it? We're not recommending that these resources be ignored; rather, we suggest that it makes sense to tailor the resources to the students' needs rather than the other way round.

If an institution prescribes a curriculum, it's still possible to introduce a learner-centered approach by developing learner-focused themes and tasks that incorporate elements of the curriculum. For example, the curriculum may require students to learn the past tense of irregular verbs. At the same time, the goals negotiated with the learners may include telling about personal histories, making travel arrangements, dealing with children's schools and dealing with community problems such as reporting a theft to police.

Learning the past tense of irregular verbs fits very well into these and other topics. When recounting personal histories, learners might wish to talk about how they came to the country. In doing so, they would need to use the past tense of irregular verbs to say things like, "1 came here six months ago," and "I brought my three children with me." In this way, virtually any prescribed curriculum requirement can be incorporated naturally into a learner-centered approach.

Keeping careful records helps us track the prescribed items students have learned and provides a basis for reviewing and extending their skills in the context of other topics. We can also check off the items on the curriculum document itself. Procedures such as these help ensure that we fulfill the institution's requirements while meeting learners' needs.

Conclusion

Both the teacher and the learners bring expertise to the language-learning process. The teacher is an expert in language-learning, planning collaboratively and engaging students in learning activities. The learners' expertise arises from their personal backgrounds and involves their knowledge of how they need to use language to attain their personal goals.

Assessing needs and negotiating curriculum are very important elements of the learning process because they enable us to get to know students quickly, create a flexible overall plan based on the goals that have been negotiated, design tasks that both accommodate the students' learning styles and build on their strengths, and make choices among different kinds of activities.

For these reasons, we recommend undertaking the challenging process of assessing needs and negotiating curriculum, a process requiring both students and teacher to take risks and compromise. It will never result in a perfect plan, but it does enable us to create one that respects the needs of all students and meets at least some of their needs.

This chapter outlined why and how to assess needs and negotiate curriculum; the next describes how we plan a program based on the results of these processes.

. . . .

PLANNING UNITS

The themes identified during the needs assessment process conducted when classes begin become the focus of units for students. Planning by units helps us create an organized structure for a course, strengthening the continuity of our teaching and helping us keep communicative purposes central.

The unit-planning process involves identifying key tasks that students want to be able to perform in the real world. It also involves making decisions about both the skills students need to perform these tasks successfully and how these skills can be developed.

What Is a Unit?

Within a course, the units focus on communicative needs identified as themes during the needs assessment process. A unit provides a framework for several lessons related to a particular theme. The number of lessons required to complete each unit depends on several factors:

— The range and difficulty of the content.
— The potential for language-learning.
— The level of student interest.
— The length of the course.

Approaches

In general, we define units according to their organizing principle: project-based, content-based or topic-based.

— Project-based units focus on learning language and content in the context of completing a specific project. Projects typically have a concrete outcome, such as completing a travel plan or producing a recipe book.
— Content-based units focus on learning the language necessary to explore a specific body of information or ideas. Learners seek, exchange and apply information and ideas on a particular subject. Examples of content-based units include learning about AIDS prevention, current events or citizenship requirements.
— Topic-based units focus on learning the language necessary to perform tasks related to a specific area of life. Topic-based units might include housing, jobs and food.

These three organizing principles are not radically different from one another; they simply take a slightly different approach to language and content. For example, any of the three might be used equally effectively to organize a unit on a banking theme. A project-based unit might focus on creating a banking guidebook. A content-based unit might focus on learning how the banking system works, while a topic-based unit might focus on actual banking transactions. The choice of focus is based on students' needs and abilities.

We do not recommend using grammar as the organizing principle for units. In other words, if students need help with forming the past tense of verbs, we suggest that this be taught in the context of the communicative tasks involved in project-, content- and topic-based units. Organizing units around grammar principles focuses on the forms of language and tends to ignore meaning-making and language use.

Why Organize by Units?

The structure provided by using units as the overall organizing principle of a course enables us to help students use and practice language in meaningful ways. Here are some of the benefits:

- Communicative purposes are central.
- The needs identified during the assessment process define outcomes.
- The curriculum has continuity and coherence.
- Intensive practice of language forms occurs naturally.
- Students feel motivated.

In project-, content- and topic-based units, the students' communicative needs are central to planning, and communicative purposes are at the core of the curriculum. This clear connection to the learners' needs increases their motivation. Content, language forms, skills and strategies are integrated into units in natural ways—the ways people use language in the real world. This is what students are in our classes to learn.

Planning by units also links the needs assessment and negotiation processes to clear outcomes. It provides students with visible evidence of the impact of the needs assessment process on the curriculum, a follow-through that helps develop the teacher's credibility. Students who may have been skeptical during the needs assessment stage are often won over by evidence of its usefulness in developing a meaningful curriculum.

Furthermore, inviting students to participate in developing the unit plan encourages them to feel ownership of the learning situation. In addition, students who are used to studying from textbooks may be comforted by knowing that the curriculum does have a structure.

This structure provides the rudder that guides both the teacher and the learners toward a chosen destination. When everyone knows where they're going and how they're getting there, they can embark on the journey with confidence. When students grasp the overall goals of the course, as well as the larger purposes behind individual tasks, it increases their motivation and helps develop their understanding of how they learn language.

Planning by units also helps us assess and evaluate. We can check that the plan coincides with our philosophy and beliefs about learning. Furthermore, the goals on which the units are based also provide criteria that we—and the students—can use to assess achievement.

Organizing a course around a series of units also enables the teacher to introduce new ideas and language forms gradually, building on previously acquired knowledge and skills. This gradual introduction and re-use of new concepts, called spiralling, also helps students remember. It's easier to remember things when we can relate them to things we've learned previously—and it's easier to use language that we've practiced in a variety of contexts. As a result, students gain the confidence necessary to apply their newly learned skills in their daily lives.

Planning Units

The following case study, a unit that Julia actually used with a group of young adult students at a Canadian community college, illustrates the unit-planning process and sets the stage for the discussion that follows.

CASE STUDY: TRAVEL IN CANADA

Assessing Needs

In one of the first classes of a "level-4" course focusing on listening and speaking, a needs assessment revealed that the students were interested in travel and citizenship. As a result, a theme titled "Travel in Canada" became the third of four units included in the 14-week course. The institutional curriculum required students to learn the language needed to discuss abstract issues and begin to use information sources outside their own experience. It set out a variety of skills students were to master, including using clarification questions and recognizing relationships among ideas.

Although I completed the basic design of the unit, I asked students for feedback on the plan.

Identifying Resources

A survey of the resources available through the college indicated that both ESL materials and materials designed for native English speakers were available.

Fortunately, some of the ESL materials, which included both print resources and audio tapes, were at an appropriate language level. Some of them described travel experiences, while others focused on making travel arrangements.

A number of other useful resources were also available. Videos in the college library focused on various areas of the country or examined the history of various areas, although some seemed too difficult for the students. The library also had a good supply of maps. Furthermore, the college offered English-speaking volunteers who could act as conversation partners to discuss travel experiences with the ESL students.

Other teachers, too, offered helpful suggestions. These included a referral to a student travel organization and the addresses of and toll-free phone numbers for provincial tourism bureaus.

A visit to a travel agency yielded maps, schedules, price lists and glossy brochures. Phone calls to the provincial automobile association and other organizations recommended by colleagues revealed that a variety of materials—and guest speakers—were also available.

The knowledge and experience the students themselves brought to the unit was also an important consideration. For example, they had considerable travel experience, mostly overseas. My own travel experience, both within Canada and overseas, was also extensive.

Deciding on an Organizing Principle

A project-based unit was selected for the following reasons:

— The students seemed highly motivated by concrete outcomes.
— It would involve students in using language for real purposes as they gathered information by interacting with one another and members of the community.
— It would give students the knowledge they wanted about travel opportunities and people and places in the country.
— The research and presentation skills involved were useful for these particular students because most of them intended to continue their formal education.

The project we settled on required students to work in groups to gather the information needed to plan a trip to a particular area. To do this, they needed to develop an itinerary within specified cost and time constraints. The groups were to make a presentation to the class, focusing on information about the area they had selected and describing their itinerary.

Identifying Key Real-World Tasks

The initial needs assessment helped identify several key real-world tasks involved in the unit:

— Gathering information about places and travel opportunities from travel experts, friends and print, audio and visual materials.
— Negotiating travel plans with peers.
— Presenting descriptive information and travel plans to the whole class.

Identifying Skills and Content

To analyze the skills students needed to work on, I did the tasks myself and identified the kinds of knowledge and skills that seemed to be needed. I also conducted more detailed needs assessments with the students; as they performed some of the key tasks, I observed to identify common areas of difficulty.

This process revealed that the unit could involve students in learning:

— *Content*: Information about places; sources of information about places.
— *Cultural information*: Information about the travel reservation system; information about the kinds of vacations popular among the students' English-speaking peers.
— *Vocabulary*: Language of travel (e.g., flight, non-stop, return, reserve, book); language of accommodation (e.g., room service, motel, hotel, campground); language of geography (e.g., prairie, harbor, peninsula).
— *Grammar*: Use of verbs of intention (e.g., intend to, plan to, hope to); use of polite question forms; use of irregular past tense verbs; use of modals to express possibility (e.g., might, could); use of "go" and "come," "bring" and "take"; use of "if" (future possible); use of "it" and "there" as dummy subjects (e.g., It takes three hours…, There is a great ski area…).
— *Body language*: How we show that we're listening; eye contact used when asking questions.

— *Pronunciation skills*: Syllable stress and unstress in place names; intonation in clarification questions.
— *Compensatory strategies*: Clarifying comprehension (e.g., Did you say…?); requesting repetition.
— *Language functions*: Agreeing and disagreeing; comparing and contrasting; describing a place; describing a location; describing a sequence of events; expressing preference; requesting information.
— *Skills*: Listening, speaking and reading—little writing required.
— *Language-use strategies*: Identifying key information while listening; making a planned presentation to a group; participating in problem-solving group discussion.

Clearly, we didn't have time to concentrate on every one of these elements. Furthermore, the students already possessed many of these skills to some degree. As a result, when planning the unit, we worked together to select specific areas of focus.

Identifying Tasks and Preparing a Unit Outline

The following is a summary of the communicative tasks identified as important in the unit, as well as the enabling skills needed to complete each successfully. Notice that the first few tasks are designed to activate students' previous knowledge and to introduce important language forms and knowledge needed to complete the project. This lays the groundwork for the later tasks.

Travel in Canada—Unit Outline

Students will—	Enabling skills required
Listen for key information in reports on trips people have taken	Travel vocabulary Time sequence Listening for key information
Tell about trips they have taken	Travel vocabulary Verbs: go-come, bring-take "It" and "there" as dummy subjects

Travel in Canada—Unit Outline

Students will—	Enabling skills required
Listen to national weather forecasts and record key information	Stressed and unstressed syllables Place names
Complete paired information-gap tasks identifying the names and locations of provinces and important cities	Language of geographical location Stressed and unstressed syllables
Form groups of three and choose a province or territory of interest to the group	Expressing preference
Find out about the area selected—phone tourism bureaus for information and interview people who have visited the area	Polite question forms Verbs: intend to, plan to, hope to Asking for clarification
Gather travel information—talk to travel agencies and student travel representatives, scan print materials from the library, tourism bureaus and travel agencies	Polite question forms Verbs: intend to, plan to, hope to Clarification questions Interpreting body language
Negotiate with group members about spending travel budget—what to see and do	Agreeing and disagreeing Future possible conditional Comparing Verbs: might, could
Present information about the area and their travel plans, including visuals and budget information	Planning presentations Speaking and presentation skills Responding to questions
Gather key information from presentations of other groups	Listening for key information Asking for clarification

Establishing Evaluation Criteria

The planning process included provisions for continuously monitoring both the effectiveness of the unit and the students' progress. Short sessions to discuss both the progress of the unit and changes group members wished to make were scheduled every week throughout the unit. The first column of the following chart lists the evaluation tasks that were used to assess students' achievement as the unit drew to a close; the second outlines the evaluation criteria used for each task.

Evaluation

Tasks	Criteria
In pairs, students role-play getting information from a travel agent	Desired information is communicated Appropriate use of polite question forms Appropriate use of clarification questions

As groups negotiate travel plan, teacher observes each group and gives feedback	Participation of individuals
	Correctness of forms
	    future conditional
	    agreeing and disagreeing
	    expressing preference
	    might, could

In middle and at end of negotiation process, students evaluate group process and their own performance	Active participation of all members Expressing and supporting opinions Body language Level of formality
Presenters, audience and teacher evaluate presentations	Clarity of key information Organization Effective use of visuals Effective use of language forms focused on during unit
Teacher and presenters evaluate audience	Accuracy of information recorded Appropriateness of clarification questions Listening body language

As the unit unfolded, the original plan was modified somewhat. We found that we needed not only to work on some enabling skills that we hadn't planned, but also to drop a few we had planned because of time constraints. Nevertheless, the unit was productive as well as enjoyable; the students learned useful language and content and enhanced their overall language development.

By reducing the scope and complexity of the tasks, a similar unit could also work with students whose English skills are less advanced. It might focus on planning a field trip for the class or planning trips to places of interest in the community. The key real-world tasks might be limited to such things as phoning for bus information, looking at brochures and discussing options with classmates. The presentation might involve groups in giving the class instructions about scheduling and transportation for the event.

A Process for Unit-Planning

As the case study illustrated, the unit-planning process involves a number of steps. These steps are not, however, discrete stages in a linear process. In fact, they often overlap and may not be completed in the same order every time. For example, although we typically begin with a needs assessment, we return to this stage again and again, both during the planning process and as the unit unfolds.

One of the most important elements of the planning process is the students' involvement, though this varies according to their needs, abilities and tolerance for planning activities. Nevertheless, it's important to encourage them to become as involved as possible in order to help them take responsibility for their own learning.

When planning, we keep in mind several important principles. First, we try to plan the unit so that students experience success along the way. This can be achieved by:

— Limiting the number of new skills required to perform any task.
— Providing opportunities for intensive practice.
— Spiralling new skills so that they are practiced in many contexts.
— Using the four skills of listening, speaking, reading and writing to support one another.
— Introducing new material in a variety of ways to accommodate varied learning styles.

Second, we try to provide students with as many opportunities as possible to use real language in real contexts by developing tasks that require them to really communicate with classmates and others. As noted in the first chapter, using language to make meaning is crucial to effective learning. Furthermore, research shows that students often learn unexpected things from language-learning tasks. We can't always accurately predict what students are ready to learn at a given time. Communicative practice provides them with opportunities to learn both what they can and what they need.

Another issue worth considering is whether all the students in the class should be assigned the same tasks. Students come to class with different needs, interests and abilities and there may be times when it makes sense to tailor activities to specific individuals or groups. The issue of individualizing the plan is discussed in the chapter titled "Putting Plans into Action."

It also makes sense to provide a variety of tasks or activities. This not only keeps the class interesting but also maximizes learning opportunities. This doesn't mean that a task should never be repeated; in fact, some repetition of both skills and procedures is often reassuring for students.

The unit plan represents an overall blueprint, identifying the order of key communicative tasks, skills and content development. Individual lessons and tasks are not planned in detail until we are actually working on the unit with the students. This is because creating detailed plans sometimes makes it difficult to maintain flexibility. As a unit unfolds, students often want and need more work on some skills—and less work on others. As a result, it's sometimes necessary to change the emphasis or direction. Carefully laid plans can become a burden; the time and energy we have invested can make us reluctant to make the changes necessary.

ASSESSING NEEDS

The needs assessment process discussed in the previous chapter helps us plan and work on the unit. First, we work with the students to identify themes of interest to the group. Second, we explore these themes in more detail, identifying key communicative tasks as well as the students' abilities, knowledge, attitudes and learning styles and the way they relate to these tasks.

To complete any unit successfully, we must consider the resources available both in the community and within the institution. It's important to use community resources because these are the real-world materials students want to be able to deal with. Sometimes called authentic materials, these resources include the media (e.g., newspapers, films, radio and TV, books, and promotional and public education materials), people who can visit the classroom (e.g., English-speaking volunteers and agency representatives), and places students can visit (e.g, stores and museums).

Although some of these materials may seem out-of-reach for students whose English is limited, they can, nevertheless, be used successfully if students are well-prepared and the tasks are broken down into manageable segments. For example, while students may not be able to understand an entire newspaper article, they may be able to find key information or circle familiar words. The students involved in the case study were unable to understand all the information in the travel brochures, but they could identify key information and use the pictures to get a sense of the places being discussed. Successful interactions with real English-language materials are highly motivating for students.

Most ESL departments offer resources designed especially for students who are learning English. These usually include commercial materials, such as textbooks and audio and videotapes, as well as materials prepared by other teachers. Many of us also design our own materials. While this enables us to tailor the materials to a particular group of students, it is time-consuming and sometimes costly.

Don't forget that the students themselves are often an excellent source of resources. We've found that the materials they bring to class are usually geared to their ability level and relevant to their needs.

As discussed earlier, another important resource is the knowledge and expertise of both the teacher and the students. For example, if students are accomplished cooks, this will affect the approach taken to a unit on cooking. This principle was used in planning the unit illustrated in the case study. Because the students had lots of travel experience, the first part of the unit invited them to tell about trips they had taken.

In doing this, students not only activated their previous knowledge of travel and travel language, but also practiced relating their own experiences, something they wanted to do in their daily lives.

DECIDING ON AN ORGANIZING PRINCIPLE

Once a theme of interest is identified, we need to decide on the organizing principle for the unit. The first step in this process involves clarifying the unit's goals. Then we think about which approach—project-based, content-based or topic-based—is most appropriate. Which would most effectively meet the unit's goals? When making this decision, we find it helpful to consider the level of student motivation, the availability of resources, our preferred teaching style, students' learning styles, the potential for successfully learning useful language and content, and the potential for using language in real contexts when completing the tasks involved.

IDENTIFYING KEY REAL-WORLD TASKS

After settling on the approach, we can identify the key real-world tasks the students will work on over the course of the unit. A real-world task is a communicative activity that involves learners in actively making meaning for authentic purposes. They are "key" because they are the tasks the students want to complete in the real world.

The needs assessment plays an important role in identifying these real-world tasks. At this time, it's important to consider not only what the students want to be able to do, but also their abilities and their potential for achieving the goals identified.

Most units include only a few key real-world tasks, such as gathering information in order to make a decision or filling in an application form in order to get a job. While only a limited number of real-world tasks may be identified, the unit includes many communicative activities designed to help students learn to complete these tasks successfully.

IDENTIFYING SKILLS AND CONTENT

After identifying the key real-world tasks, we consider what students need to learn in order to complete these tasks successfully. To do this, we need to analyze the tasks as they are actually completed in specific contexts in the real world. If the tasks involve conversation, for example, we might record and analyze actual conversations. While it's possible—and certainly convenient—to simply visualize conversations, this strategy must be used with caution. It's easy to imagine conversations quite differently from the way they actually happen. Furthermore, our own experience may not match the contexts in which ESL students need to use language. For example, the language used to give instructions on a construction site may be quite different from the language used to do the same thing in a different workplace.

Writing tasks can be analyzed by examining authentic samples of writing appropriate to the task. For example, if the students need to learn to write résumés in order to apply for jobs, we might ask to look over the résumés of people we know. Again, however, it's important to be aware of the context. The résumé of someone looking for a teaching job may be very different from that of someone looking for another kind of job. In fact, a résumé is entirely unnecessary when applying for some jobs.

Readings and taped listening activities can be analyzed by examining the language, organization and content of the material. When doing this, a variety of factors affecting students' understanding of the material must be considered. These include content knowledge, cultural information, vocabulary, grammar, body language, pronunciation skills, compensatory strategies, language functions, skills (listening, speaking, reading and writing) and language-use strategies.

Although this analysis may seem difficult at first, it gets easier with practice. If an important enabling skill is missed, it will become apparent when students are unable to complete a task. At that point, the activities can be adjusted to include work on the skill needed.

A list of the skills students need to learn can also be developed by inviting them to role-play the key tasks. Elements of this process are described in the following chapter, as well as in the chapter titled "Assessing Needs and Negotiating Curriculum." Observe the students as they role-play the tasks, note where they're having trouble, and design activities to help them improve their skills in these areas.

In many cases, time constraints prevent us from dealing with every area flagged for work. This means that we must be selective in deciding which skills to focus on. A number of questions must be taken into account when making these decisions:

— What skills are absolutely necessary if students are to complete the tasks successfully?
— What skills are required by the institutional curriculum?
— What skills would be useful in other contexts of interest to the students?
— What skills worked on in previous units can be usefully reviewed or extended?
— What skills will students need to complete tasks in future units?
— What skills do students need to enhance their overall language development?

IDENTIFYING TASKS AND PREPARING A UNIT OUTLINE

The tasks involved in this stage of the process fall into two categories. The first includes enabling tasks, which help students develop the skills needed to complete the key real-world tasks successfully. These often deal with aspects of content, culture, grammar, vocabulary or the sound system.

The second category involves tasks that approximate or replicate real-world tasks. In the case study, for example, one of the enabling tasks involved providing intensive practice of the language forms used to express preference. The skill focused on in the enabling task was then used in the more authentic task of making a decision about which geographical area the group would study.

The unit outline is exactly that—an outline that sets out, in general terms, the learning tasks that students will be invited to complete over the course of the unit.

ESTABLISHING EVALUATION CRITERIA

Evaluation is most effective when it is tied to the goals of the unit. As part of the planning process, we suggest working with the students to decide how both the unit and their achievement will be evaluated.

The evaluation process involves three elements. All three incorporate self-evaluation by both the teacher and the learners, as well as the learners' evaluation of the teacher's work and the teacher's evaluation of the learners' work.

— Evaluate students' progress toward their goals while the unit is in progress. The purpose of this evaluation is to help the group modify the plan in response to emerging needs.
— Evaluate students' achievement at the end of the unit and, when appropriate, at specified points over the course of the unit. This process not only enhances the students' motivation and achievement, but may also be required by the institution. It involves developing a formal record of the students' achievements.
— Evaluate the process and product of the unit in order to guide further planning. This is important not only for planning future units with the same group, but also for our development as teachers.

What Should a Unit Include?

Like the process of planning a unit, the process of developing the components of a unit is not linear. As the unit is completed, the various elements are visited and revisited many times.

DEVELOPING THE CONTEXT

When teaching a unit, it's important to orient the learners to its context. This helps activate their previous knowledge, which includes not only language forms but also information and cultural knowledge. Orienting students to the theme increases their motivation and is consistent with our philosophy of the prime importance of making meaning.

COMPLETING A UNIT-SPECIFIC NEEDS ASSESSMENT

In addition to the general needs assessment that identified the theme and organizing principle of the unit, it's important to complete a more specific assessment of the students' learning needs either just before or very soon after the unit begins. The purpose of this assessment is to identify the students' abilities and needs in relation to the specific unit. An example of a unit-specific assessment is shown on page 28. Needs assessment procedures sometimes also have an orientation function.

unit-specific assessment is shown on page 28.

DEVELOPING ENABLING SKILLS AND KNOWLEDGE

The teacher's role is to help students develop the skills and knowledge they need to function in the real world. These skills are taught most effectively by introducing activities that involve students in using particular language forms to make meaning. For example, past tense verbs might be practiced in the context of reporting on an experience the class shared.

FOSTERING A "SAFE" ENVIRONMENT

Students thrive when they have an opportunity to practice new skills in an environment that encourages them to feel comfortable about experimenting and making mistakes. For many adult students, especially those who were educated in systems where different philosophies prevail, this does not come easily.

> *Julia*: As a new teacher, I was told by one student that I was the nicest English teacher he had ever had. Needless to say, I was thrilled. Later, it came out that his only other experience with an English teacher was in his home country. That teacher hit him whenever he made a mistake.

Clearly, helping students feel comfortable about making mistakes is a challenging task in some cases. Strategies that help do this are discussed in the chapter titled "Putting Plans into Action."

Students also need opportunities to practice their new skills in ways that help them build confidence in their abilities. We can promote this by designing tasks that limit the scope for error, at least at first. For example, the tasks may include a limited choice of language forms. As students' competence grows and their new skills are integrated into the language they already know, the level of control over the tasks can be progressively reduced.

Completing key tasks in the safe environment of the classroom is also important because it provides students with intensive practice and opportunities to learn from one another. As teachers, we need to be creative in developing tasks that provide repeated, yet stimulating, practice.

PRACTICING KEY TASKS IN THE REAL WORLD

Moving beyond the classroom to complete "contact" tasks in the real world is an important aspect of developing students' skills. By completing contact tasks in the real world, students have an opportunity to apply their newly learned skills in their daily lives. Specific suggestions for developing contact tasks are discussed in the following chapter.

COMPLETING RELATED TASKS

Students also need opportunities to apply their newly acquired skills to a range of tasks. For example, if they have been working on giving information about themselves in a unit on applying for jobs, they might also apply these skills in other situations, such as opening a bank account or applying for a credit card. Often called extension, this spiralling of tasks helps students practice their skills. It also shows them how the skills they've learned apply in a broader context.

EVALUATING ACHIEVEMENT

Although achievement is monitored throughout the unit, we also try to design some activities for the specific purpose of evaluating both students' progress and the effectiveness of the unit. While this evaluation can certainly take the form of a traditional written test, other activities often provide a more accurate measure of students' learning.

No matter what activities are eventually settled on, it's important for students to be aware of the evaluation criteria. For example, the criteria for a conversation task might assess the success of the communication, the fluency of speech, the responsiveness to the other participant, and the accuracy of the forms that were the focus of the unit. Although criteria like these require the teacher to make subjective judgments, they give a more accurate picture of the students' communicative abilities than paper-and-pencil tests.

Conclusion

Planning by units enables us to create a flexible framework for sections of a course, though it's worth noting that the specific elements of the process vary from one unit to another and one teacher to another.

When evaluating a unit plan, we consider a number of issues. First, we try to ensure that it is based on the students' authentic language needs and that it provides as many opportunities as possible to use language for authentic communicative purposes. Second, we consider its contribution to the students' overall language development. Does it build on and extend their previous knowledge and the skills they already possess? Third, we ensure that the unit includes opportunities for students to acquire and use new skills in a variety of contexts for a variety of purposes. Finally, we consider the level of detail included in the plan. We try to ensure that there is enough to serve as a useful guide, but not so much that we are discouraged from changing it as the need arises.

Implicit in this discussion is the concept that learning tasks are the basic building blocks of units. In the following chapter, we explore a variety of tasks used in language teaching.

. . . .

DEVELOPING TASKS

Just as the themes that make up the curriculum are based on the needs identified during the assessment process, so too are the specific tasks that make up the units. This chapter focuses on developing tasks designed to help students achieve their communicative goals.

We all use language to achieve communicative goals, which revolve around ensuring that our needs are met. These needs may be physical—for food, clothing, shelter and safety—or social and psychological—to make friends and feel respected, for example, or to learn and enrich our lives, perhaps by extending our job training or enjoying music.

In order to meet our needs, we must perform a variety of tasks that may include:

— Gathering information (e.g., the time the bus leaves).
— Expressing ideas (e.g., the rights of tenants), opinions (e.g., the best place to live) and attitudes (e.g., the importance of the family).
— Articulating feelings (e.g., the way we feel when someone is rude).
— Making judgments (e.g., the way we want to educate our children).

A knowledge of the specific needs—and communicative goals—of the adult ESL students in our classes and the communication tasks that arise from them is crucial in making decisions not only about *what* to teach but also about *how* to teach it.

Real-World Tasks and Enabling Tasks

The previous chapter described two kinds of learning tasks—real-world tasks and enabling tasks. When completing real-world tasks, students use their skills to achieve real adult purposes. To help them do this, we try to create classroom conditions that replicate real-world situations and require students to integrate their skills and knowledge to achieve authentic goals. Enabling tasks, on the other hand, help students develop the skills and knowledge they need to successfully complete real-world tasks. Enabling tasks typically isolate particular aspects of language for intensive practice.

We recommend making both real-world and enabling tasks as communicative as possible. In the past, for example, many teachers taught grammar by using exercises in which meaning was unimportant, such as following a pattern by adding *ed* to verbs. As a result, students were often unable to transfer the grammar skills they'd mastered while completing the exercises to situations in which they needed to use language to achieve real purposes. If students use meaningful language while completing enabling tasks, however, they are more likely to be able to transfer their learning to real-world situations.

Another way to look at tasks is to distinguish between those that focus on helping students develop fluency and those that focus on using language accurately. Fluency refers to the speed and efficiency of communication, as well as the ability to use a range of language. Accuracy refers to students' ability to use language correctly, according to accepted conventions of grammar, syntax, the sound system and vocabulary.

Both enabling and real-world tasks can help develop students' fluency and accuracy. Real-world tasks help develop fluency by requiring students to integrate their skills in the ways demanded by real life. Because enabling tasks often focus on particular language forms, they help improve accuracy. However, they can also help develop fluency; as students engage in intensive practice, they have opportunities to develop fluent responses to situations.

It is the teacher's responsibility to find ways of integrating communicative purposes into the tasks we invite students to perform. Even when the students need to focus on language forms in order to facilitate learning, it is possible to integrate communicative purposes into the activities. Here is one way of doing this:

— Select a manageable, authentic purpose for using language based on the needs identified (e.g., look at a food-store flier and choose something you want to buy).
— Focus on and practice the language forms students need to master in order to achieve this purpose (e.g., count and non-count nouns, such as "oranges" and "rice").
— Encourage them to use these language forms accurately to achieve a more complex authentic purpose (e.g., use the flier to question a partner about the cost of various foods—"How much are oranges?").

Choosing Tasks

Like the tasks adults perform in the real world, the tasks students perform in class vary widely, depending on their purpose, setting and content, the attitudes, roles and relationships of the participants, and the skills and strategies needed to perform them successfully. Furthermore, while learning tasks have a communicative purpose, they also have a learning purpose such as:

— To activate students' previous knowledge (e.g., brainstorm street names).
— To recognize similarities and differences (e.g., the difference between the intonation of questions and statements; the similarities between cultures).
— To produce language (e.g., use correct intonation when asking a question).
— To identify a new concept (e.g., use examples to figure out a rule, such as when to use "a" before a noun).
— To use a new concept (e.g., apply a rule to specific cases).
— To practice (e.g., use language in a communicative activity).
— To review (e.g., practice at a later time).
— To extend (e.g., practice the new skill in other communicative situations).
— To understand the language-learning process (e.g., understand strategies for developing vocabulary independently).

— To build confidence (e.g., use language to achieve real-life goals).
— To assess needs (e.g., identify need to develop ability to disagree).
— To build group rapport (e.g., get to know more about one another).

When planning tasks or choosing among tasks set out in published materials, it's helpful to keep the following principles in mind:

— Make students aware of the purposes—both communicative and learning—of the tasks by involving them in the planning process and discussing the reasons for completing the tasks.
— Use authentic adult tasks (activities and materials) frequently. Make the tasks as communicative as possible and avoid tasks that the learners may perceive as childish, such as games that make them feel foolish.
— Keep tasks short. To help students remain stimulated and maintain concentration and reduce frustration, use a variety of short, related tasks rather than one long one.
— Plan tasks in relation to one another. Build from simpler to more complex tasks and from more controlled to less controlled tasks. Vary groupings, skills and activities.
— Ensure that students will be successful by limiting the amount of new material introduced (e.g., eight to 10 new vocabulary items is plenty), maximizing opportunities for students to practice and integrate new skills, and trying the task before expecting the students to complete it.

Kinds of Tasks

The tasks presented in the following material are intended only as a starting point. ESL textbooks and the resources listed under "Additional Reading" also provide ideas.

The communicative potential and authenticity of the tasks vary. Those outlined first tend to be more difficult to design as communicative tasks than those presented later. The earlier tasks also tend to be less cognitively demanding because they are more controlled, requiring students to integrate fewer aspects of language. They are also more likely to become repetitive and boring. As the discussion progresses, the tasks become more naturally student-centered and more similar to authentic adult tasks.

REPETITION TASKS

When completing these tasks, students repeat specific language forms—words, phrases or sentences. While repetition tasks are rarely communicative, they can be useful enabling tasks, particularly for developing pronunciation skills and learning expressions. Because of their lack of communicative potential, however, it's a good idea to use them sparingly.

Here is a suggested procedure for carrying out a word-repetition task:

— Help students understand the meaning of the word (e.g., show a picture or gesture, or give a synonym).
— Say the word.
— Encourage students to say and repeat the word as a group and individually.
— Use the word in a meaningful sentence.
— Encourage students to repeat the sentence.
— Use the word in a communicative activity.

When dealing with long words or sentences that students have trouble repeating all at once, building back from the end is a good idea. For example, take the sentence, "How many hours a week do you work?" Begin by asking students to repeat a manageable segment at the end—"do you work?" Gradually add the segments that precede it—"hours a week do you work?"—until they can repeat the entire sentence.

Building back from the end is more effective than starting at the beginning of the sentence because it's easier to maintain natural intonation and stress.

DICTATION TASKS

This involves reading a passage aloud as students write what they hear. In some cases, it helps to introduce some of the words ahead of time. Although dictation is hardly an authentic activity, it can be a useful learning task. Among other things, it helps students improve their listening skills and writing accuracy. Keep dictations short—as little as one sentence for students who are just beginning to learn English to no more than five or six sentences for students whose English skills are more proficient.

When giving a dictation, read aloud the selected passage three times. The first time, read normally as students listen for meaning. The second, break the passage into segments that learners are likely to be able to remember and record. Ensure that they have enough time to write and try not to distort the speed or intonation. Read normally the third time, pausing briefly between sentences so students can correct their work.

If dictations are used as an assessment activity, they can be collected and checked. However, if they are used as learning activities, encourage students to check their own work. They might work together to try to come up with a perfect transcription, or individuals might write parts of the passage on the chalkboard for discussion. This may involve copying their own work or dictating a segment to another student who writes it on the chalkboard. After going over the passage, be sure to read it again so students can hear what they missed.

MATCHING TASKS

These tasks involve matching meanings, forms or structures—pictures with text, words with other words (synonyms, antonyms or definitions), questions with answers, or phrases with other phrases. Although they are more concerned with meaning than repetition tasks, their purposes are rarely communicative. Still, they can be useful for developing vocabulary and grammar skills.

Here is a typical matching task:

Write the letter from Column 2 beside the words in Column 1 that have a similar meaning. The first one is done for you.

Column 1	Column 2
b. Just a minute.	a. I don't know.
She's not here.	b. Hang on.
Is Maria there?	c. Could you repeat that?
Pardon me?	d. She's not in.
I'm not sure.	e. Can I speak to Maria?

To complete these tasks, students must place a series of sentences or words in order. Although ordering tasks are not authentic, they can help students recognize both the way text is organized and the words and phrases that indicate relationships between ideas such as cause and effect and time sequence.

This is a typical sequence for completing a sentence-ordering task:

— Write each sentence of a paragraph on a separate strip of paper. Try to choose a paragraph that sets out a reasonably clear sequence of events or ideas.
— Divide the class into small groups and give each a set of sentences.
— Ask the groups to arrange the sentences in a logical sequence.

Placing words in order within a sentence is usually used to help students understand and practice English word order, although this kind of enabling task is low on the communicative scale.

COMPLETION TASKS

These tasks require students to complete a partial text. While the text may be a sentence or story, it may also be a chart or outline that students are expected to complete after listening to or reading a passage.

Sentence completion activities are often used to help students use particular structures to express their own meanings. For example, students might be asked to complete a statement like this: "If I lost my wallet, I...."

Although these tasks can be worthwhile, they are too frequently presented without any context, so that students end up making sentences for the purpose of making sentences rather than for communicative purposes.

Cloze passages are a kind of completion task. In some cases, cloze involves deleting words from a passage at specified intervals (often every fifth, seventh or ninth word). Students then fill in the missing words. Another version of cloze involves deleting specific categories of words, such as nouns or adjectives, and asking students to fill in words that make sense in the context. While cloze tasks can help assess students' overall language development, their potential as learning tasks is limited.

Many traditional grammar exercises are essentially completion tasks that require learners to fill in blanks with correct words or word forms. These exercises can be useful in drawing students' attention to particular grammar issues, but they need to be developed as communicative activities. Recently published grammar textbooks, such as those by Betty Azar and Diane Larsen-Freeman, are a considerable improvement over previous books because the exercises are presented in a context and have some communicative value.

Substitution drills, another kind of completion task, present students with a sample sentence and ask them to replace part of it with other words. These tasks provide intensive practice with structures or vocabulary and help extend the use of language forms to other situations. Although they are often presented with no communicative purpose, it is possible to design drills that are communicative.

Here's how a substitution drill might be tailored to the needs of students who are concerned about finding housing:

— The teacher presents a model sentence (e.g., I'm looking for a one-bedroom apartment).
— Students repeat the sentence.
— The teacher says a new word or shows a picture representing a new word (e.g., two-bedroom, studio, etc.).
— The students say the sentence, substituting the new word for a word in the model sentence (e.g., I'm looking for a two-bedroom apartment).
— Present and substitute other words in the same way.

These drills can be effective if the language forms are subsequently used in communicative tasks.

INFORMATION-GAP TASKS

Information-gap tasks require students to get or give information. They can get information by reading or listening, looking at maps, graphs or pictures, or drawing on their own life experiences. They can give information by speaking, writing, drawing or role-playing. Here, we discuss three kinds of information-gap tasks: comprehension tasks; two-way information-gap tasks; and jigsaw tasks.

Comprehension tasks, which require students to read or listen so that they can answer comprehension questions, are the most basic form of information-gap task. Here is a suggested procedure for completing comprehension tasks:

— Activate students' previous knowledge of the language and content by, for example, brainstorming to find out what they already know about the topic.
— Predict the language and content of a selected passage by discussing various clues in the text—illustrative material, headings, summaries and so on.
— Ensure that students read or listen with a purpose by asking questions ahead of time. The questions should encourage students to make inferences as well as repeat factual information. Providing them with a chart, graph, picture, map, form or other activity to complete also works well (e.g., students might read about a place and then draw a map of it).
— After reading or listening, encourage students to respond to comprehension questions.

Two-way information-gap tasks are more complex because they require students to work in pairs. Each student has different information and, to complete the task successfully, they must share their resources. For example, two students might each be given a list of prices for half the items on a shopping list. To calculate the total cost of the shopping expedition, they must share their information with each other.

Two-way tasks have several important advantages. First, they are student-centered; each student is knowledgeable, possessing information the other needs. Second, they are communicative and purposeful; completing the task successfully is clear proof that successful communication has occurred. Finally, students have a chance to negotiate meaning with each other. If communication problems arise, students are motivated to solve them by using compensatory strategies.

Jigsaw tasks are a more complex form of information-gap task that involves working in groups to communicate purposefully. As in the two-way tasks, students must share information. Here's how they work:

— Divide students into home groups of the same size (four often works well).
— Give each home group different but related information.
— Form new jigsaw groups by drawing one member from each of the home groups.
— Encourage jigsaw group members to share their information in order to complete a task.

For example, a unit on crime might include a jigsaw activity requiring students to piece together evidence from witnesses. Each home group can be given information about what one witness saw at the crime scene. The group members role-play telling their story. Then jigsaw groups are formed, drawing one member from each home group. Each witness tells the jigsaw group his or her story. Finally, the jigsaw group analyzes the information to decide who committed the crime.

BRAINSTORMING TASKS

Brainstorming, which involves students in contributing ideas or language in a non-threatening environment, is useful for activating previous knowledge and reviewing. Though it can involve the whole class, it also works well as a group activity. When brainstorming, one member acts as the scribe for the group. Here's a suggested procedure:

— As group members call out ideas, the scribe lists them on the chalkboard. At this stage, it's important to stress that all ideas are worthwhile and none should be dismissed. In some cases, it may be necessary for the teacher to model how to accept everyone's contribution.
— Group members discuss the ideas they collected. They may delete, change or group the ideas, or establish a list of priorities.
— The group can then use the ideas as a resource when completing other tasks, such as role-plays, described next.

ROLE-PLAY TASKS

When role-playing, students assume specific roles and act out a scenario. Role-playing encourages them to practice English in a range of situations for a variety of authentic purposes, using language to meet everyday communicative needs in the safe environment of the classroom. It is particularly useful as preparation for completing tasks that involve contact with other people.

When planning a role-play, we need to identify:

— *The setting*: Where does the role-play take place? What are the physical conditions of that place?
— *The roles*: What are the roles of the participants? What are their personalities like? How do they feel in this situation? Keep in mind that students can play themselves as well as others.
— *The situation*: What has happened just before the role-play begins? What are the objectives of the characters in this situation? When the situation involves conflict, the role-play tends to be livelier.

Here's an example of a role-play task:

— *The setting*: An electronics shop. It is a small shop in the neighborhood.
— *The roles*: Student A is a customer, playing him or herself. Student B is the shop owner who enjoys serving customers and repairing televisions.
— *The situation*: Student A's TV set doesn't work. The sound is very bad. Student A takes the set to the electronics shop. Student A wants it fixed as soon as possible because a special show is on tomorrow night. The shopkeeper is very busy.

Here's a suggested guide for developing a role-play:

— The teacher or a student describes the setting, roles and situation orally or in print. Ask the students to imagine further details.
— Students brainstorm possible developments that may occur as the scenario unfolds.
— Students brainstorm language that may be useful.
— Pairs or small groups practice the role-play without an audience.
— Students make suggestions for improving their own role-plays.
— Students present the role-play to other groups or the class.

— The audience makes suggestions for improving the role-play.
— The students practice the role-play again without an audience.
— The setting, roles or situation are changed slightly and the students perform a new role-play.

When planning role-plays, it's important to think carefully about the roles we ask students to play. For example, if the role-play involves a parent talking to his child's teacher, the teacher's role may not be manageable for the students who may not know what the teacher would say or how she would say it. Furthermore, a student who isn't a teacher probably has no need to learn to talk like a teacher. He needs only to be able to understand and respond to a teacher. Difficult, specialized roles like this should be avoided when planning role-plays.

We also need to keep in mind that some students may be reluctant to participate in role-plays. Some adults are simply shy, while others find imagining and pretending very difficult. However, role-playing is such a useful task that it's worth helping students become comfortable with it. To begin with, use simple role-plays in which students can play themselves. Later, more complex and less familiar roles and situations can be introduced.

PHYSICAL RESPONSE TASKS

These tasks involve students in responding physically to instructions or requests. These may be as simple as asking a student to close the door or as complex as inviting one student to teach another to program a VCR. When the tasks are communicative, they are satisfying for students because they provide concrete evidence of successful communication.

Care should be taken, however, not to ask students to do things they are uncomfortable with or that they would never be asked to do in the real world. It's also important to remember that students need to be able to give, as well as follow, instructions.

JOURNAL-WRITING TASKS

Journal-writing, which involves students in creating a written record of their experiences, helps develop writing fluency. A strategy that is typically uncontrolled or minimally controlled, it can be used to help students reflect on the outcomes of learning tasks or activate previous knowledge. Diaries, language-experience journals and learning journals are three kinds of journals that can be used effectively.

Describing their daily activities in a diary can be useful practice for students who are just beginning to learn English. They can write about what they did, how they felt and what they saw.

For students whose English is more proficient, language-experience journals and learning journals are often more useful options. In language-experience journals, students report on and respond to their experiences with using English. Journals like this encourage students to use English outside the classroom and provide them with an opportunity to write reflectively about their experiences of language use.

> *Julia*: I encourage students in a listening class to watch TV programs and write about them in their journals. The students describe their reasons for choosing the program, the basic content, their reaction, and their successes and problems in understanding the show.
>
> A colleague invites students to use journals to report on their experiences with conversations in English. They describe the participants, purpose and content of the conversations, as well as their difficulties and successes.

In learning journals, students write about their developing understanding of English and their new culture. Their writing may include their insights into, confusion over and experiences of language and culture both inside and outside the classroom. For this to be successful, it may be necessary to help them develop the vocabulary needed to talk about language, language-learning and culture. These journals can help us plan useful learning tasks and help students think about and understand their skills, knowledge and learning processes.

Journal-writing is most effective when it is done frequently, at least twice a week. An important element of the process is the teacher's responses, which are also recorded in the journals. Because responding to students' writing can be very time-consuming, it's worth remembering that the emphasis of journal-writing is on communicating ideas and gaining fluency. As a result, focusing on language forms isn't appropriate.

Instead, quickly read through the journal entries and respond to the content in one or two sentences. Language form should be noted only when it interferes with understanding or when students ask specific questions about it.

Confidentiality is also an important issue. Because students sometimes record private thoughts, we must respect their right to privacy and share the contents of the journals with others only with permission.

DISCUSSION TASKS

Discussion tasks, which involve students in sharing opinions, ideas and feelings, are authentic activities that adults engage in frequently in their daily lives. While these tasks are most effective for developing fluency and strategies for interacting with others, the teacher's feedback can also make them useful for improving accuracy. Discussion activities can range from simple idea-sharing with a partner to more formal discussions involving the whole class.

Successful discussions share these qualities:

— A clear purpose (e.g., sharing perspectives on an issue or identifying points of agreement and disagreement).
— The participants respond to one another and respect one another's ideas.
— Clear outcomes (e.g., a summary of ideas).

Reviewing the roles and responsibilities of participants improves the quality of discussions. They work best when participants take responsibility for ensuring that everyone has an opportunity to contribute, keeping the discussion going, responding to the ideas of others, supporting their opinions, and exploring ideas in depth. Formal discussions often involve a leader who facilitates by asking questions and following up on the contributions of participants. While the teacher may take this role initially, it's important to encourage students to lead their own discussions.

Here is a suggested procedure for organizing a discussion with a leader:

Before the discussion:

— Identify or plan a common experience for participants. This may be an activity shared by the class, such as a field trip, a short reading or a video, or something the students have in common, such as the experience of immigration or of dealing with landlords.

— Clearly define the issue and identify a focus for the discussion. For example, a field trip to the courthouse might provide a choice of issues: whether an accused person was guilty or innocent; the treatment of witnesses; or how the courthouse building reflects our culture. If students are aware of the focus ahead of time, they will be able to gather their thoughts on the issue and participate more actively.

During the discussion:

— Raise questions to open the discussion. Effective questions are open-ended; there is no single correct answer. The leader's opinion should not be implied or stated in the question; for example, "What do you think of X?" is preferable to "Don't you think X is a bad idea?"

— Ensure that everyone has an opportunity to participate. Some students may be reluctant to participate because of lack of interest, fear of speaking out in English, or personal or cultural communication styles. As a result, it may be necessary to limit the participation of some in order to provide others with opportunities to make a contribution. Sometimes, it helps to ask quieter students whether they agree or disagree with someone else's opinion. It's also worth remembering that discussion is a listening as well as a speaking activity. Students who prefer to listen can learn much from doing so, and good listeners may be very useful as scribes. They can note important points and practice speaking by summarizing the discussion for the group.

— Draw on the experience of the participants. One of the great joys of teaching adults is that they come from diverse backgrounds and their experiences can be a wonderful resource for the group.

— Based on the responses, develop probing questions to encourage participants to examine the issues in greater depth. Useful generic probing questions include, "Can you give an example of X?" "Why do you believe X?" and "Do you think X is true in other situations?"

After the discussion:

— Recap. What points did participants agree on? What points did they disagree on? What were the reasons for the disagreement? Students can contribute this information orally or a scribe may sum up using notes. In addition to providing closure, this is also an opportunity to review key language and concepts from the discussion.

Although discussions without leaders follow much the same process, they are usually carried out in pairs or very small groups. To spark the discussion, the group can brainstorm questions ahead of time or the teacher can provide a list of questions.

PROBLEM-SOLVING TASKS

Closely related to discussion tasks are problem-solving tasks, which are also communicative and make use of adults' thinking skills. However, problem-solving tasks are usually more focused than discussion tasks because they involve students in examining a particular problem and identifying solutions.

While the problem may be logical, social, ethical or practical, the most effective problem-solving tasks are built around open-ended issues that don't have a single correct solution. The students themselves, ESL materials and the media are useful sources of ideas for problem-solving tasks.

The following sequence works well:

— In small groups, students identify the problem. It may be described in print or orally.
— Gather information.
— Analyze the information.
— Suggest solutions.
— Examine the suggested solutions critically.
— Gather in the whole group to discuss the process and results of the small-group task.

Here is an example of a problem-solving task:

A Problem at Work

Fatima works as a cashier in a large grocery store. She has worked there for three years. She likes her job. The pay is good and she likes talking to the customers. Recently, a new supervisor was transferred from another store. This new manager, a man, makes Fatima nervous. He stands too close to her. Sometimes he puts his arm around her when he's talking to her. Yesterday, he told her that the skirt of her uniform is too long. He wants her to shorten it so that it is above the knee.

1. What is the problem?
2. What do you know about Fatima's job? The place she works? Fatima's feelings?
3. What other information do you need? Ask the teacher questions about Fatima's situation.
4. What are three possible solutions to Fatima's problem? What are the pros and cons of each?
5. If you were Fatima, which solution would you try?

NEGOTIATION TASKS

These are similar to problem-solving and discussion tasks because they are communicative and encourage students to think. They also help students develop fluency in English and strategies for interacting with others. They work well with small groups and the whole class.

Negotiation tasks involve students in making decisions as a group. These decisions may be about fictitious plans, such as the trip in the case study outlined in the previous chapter, or real plans, such as a class party, field trip or unit.

When negotiating, it's important to encourage students to discuss options and support their opinions. Invariably, some students simply want to hold a vote on the options, but they get much more useful language practice if they discuss their decisions and try to reach consensus. Keep in mind that some students may need help to do this. In some cultures, disagreement is avoided at all costs; in others, disagreement is expressed much more strongly than in English.

The following is an effective procedure for carrying out a negotiation task in a small group:

— Students identify the goals of their planning.
— Identify constraints on planning.
— Gather information.
— Analyze the information.
— Suggest possible courses of action.
— State opinions about the possibilities and support them.

— Negotiate a group decision.
— Share the group's decisions and rationale with the class and, if necessary, attempt to convince others.

CONTACT TASKS

Contact tasks require students to interact with members of the community for a specific purpose. They can include a wide range of activities, such as listening to how people order food in a restaurant, asking an English-speaker the meaning of a word, saying hello to a neighbor, asking the price of an item, making an appointment, and so on.

In addition to helping students practice their newly learned skills in the community, contact tasks also fulfill a variety of other functions, such as helping students make social contact and understand cultural differences. Effective contact tasks are authentic activities with real communicative purposes.

It's important to be aware that some students are intimidated by contact tasks. The following strategies can help them overcome this fear.

— Rehearse contact tasks in class.
— Invite students to role-play contact tasks in pairs or small groups.
— Help students develop contact-task partners in the community through volunteer programs or personal acquaintances.
— Make arrangements with contact-task resource people ahead of time so that they know what is going on.
— Begin with listening tasks.
— Keep tasks short and within students' capabilities.

Choosing Resources

When developing learning tasks, teachers draw on a variety of resources—authentic materials from the real world and materials designed specifically for teaching language to ESL students. Because there are advantages and disadvantages (see the following chart) to both, it's important to achieve a balance between the two.

Authentic and ESL Materials

Authentic Materials	ESL Materials
Full range of vocabulary, structures and subject matter	Limited range of vocabulary, structures and subject matter
Both positive and negative	Overwhelmingly positive
Level of formality varies	Middle-of-the-road level of formality, little variation
Frequent use of partial sentences	Complete sentences
Faster-paced, often poorly enunciated	Slower-paced, enunciated clearly
More implied information; usually highly inferential	Less implied information; usually highly explicit

While using authentic resources helps motivate students and provides practice in dealing with the language they are likely to encounter outside the classroom, ESL materials can also be very useful. It's often easier to find accessible language that meets a wide range of needs among ESL materials. In addition, ESL textbooks typically include a range of tasks that focuses on common problem areas.

When choosing ESL materials, however, it's important to rule out those that distort the language (e.g., by using syntax that is radically different from authentic language) or are childish (e.g., stories about getting along at high school).

Conclusion

The tasks outlined in this chapter represent a range of learning activities. Some closely replicate real-world adult tasks, while others are likely to occur only in the classroom. Some, such as substitution tasks, are very controlled, providing students with little or no opportunity to make their own meanings. Others, such as problem-solving tasks, are less controlled and enable students to make their own meanings as they integrate their knowledge and skills.

The next chapter examines how we combine tasks to plan lessons for students.

. . . .

PLANNING LESSONS

The two previous chapters, which examined planning units and tasks, set the stage for this chapter, which concludes our look at planning by examining how to organize daily lessons.

Although a variety of factors—the students' needs, interests and abilities, class size, time considerations and so on—affects the way we plan effective lessons, some principles are important in nearly any context because they guide the way we select and combine tasks. This chapter explores these principles and provides a sample lesson that illustrates how they can be put into practice.

Elements of a Typical Lesson

Effective lessons tend to display certain common elements and a similar structure. They usually begin with warm-up activities followed by a sharing of the agenda for the day's session. We then move on to the specific learning tasks that form the heart of the lesson, interrupting these at an appropriate point with a break, especially when the session is long. The lesson usually ends with activities designed to bring a sense of closure to the day's efforts and help students look ahead to the next session.

Because the actual tasks vary considerably, they are discussed in detail later in the chapter. We begin with a brief examination of the other common elements of most lessons.

This is a short activity designed to introduce the session by involving students in using familiar language. Warm-up activities are worthwhile for a number of reasons:

— They provide a transition, helping students who may not have used English since the previous lesson get back to an English-speaking mindset. They also help students who may have had other things on their minds settle down to language-learning.

— They build confidence and group rapport by helping students begin the class by communicating successfully in English. They also give students a chance to relax and feel part of the group. This is particularly important at the beginning of a course or in multi-level classes where many of the learning tasks tend to separate, rather than unite, students.

— They provide time for late-arriving students to enter the class without disrupting the main learning tasks or missing key instructions.

Warm-up activities can be used to:

— Develop the context for the coming lesson (e.g., if the lesson deals with nutrition, students might work in pairs to describe what they have eaten that day).

— Revisit previous lesson or unit topics (e.g., if previous lessons dealt with banking, students might tell small groups about their latest visit to a bank).

— Help students get to know one another (e.g., students might share experiences—funny or exciting anecdotes on just about any topic likely to generate interesting stories, an activity that works best if they are prepared ahead of time).

— Have fun (e.g., the group tells a circle story: the teacher or a student provides a sentence to start things off and each student in the circle adds something).

These are just a few examples of the kinds of warm-up activities that can help get classes started on the right foot. Further suggestions can often be found in student texts.

Effective warm-up tasks:

— Give all students an opportunity to speak.

— Are short—10 minutes at most.
— Involve communicative activities.
— Require minimal instruction by the teacher.
— Are easy enough that students do not feel discouraged at the outset of the class.

Because the warm-up provides a bridge between the real world and the classroom, when planning activities we need to consider what students have done before the class and the kinds of activities they will be asked to do during the lesson. As we get to know students, planning appropriate warm-up activities becomes easier.

2. SHARING THE AGENDA

After the warm-up, students are ready to consider the plan for the day's lesson. While this component of the lesson takes only a few minutes, it is nonetheless crucial. The teacher outlines the main activities planned for the day and explains how these will help students progress toward their goals.

Making the students aware of the lesson plan has several important advantages. First, it encourages them to feel a sense of control over their learning, something that is especially important for adults. Second, when students understand what they can gain from individual tasks, it increases their motivation and helps them focus on the learning outcomes.

Sharing lesson plans is simple, but it needs some thought, particularly for beginning teachers. First, we need to consider which activities it is most useful to tell the class about. It isn't necessary to provide a detailed plan. Simply focus on the most time-consuming tasks and those that are the most communicative and authentic. Second, we need to consider how we will describe the tasks and their goals. Avoid teacher jargon and try to relate the information to the students' lives. Finally, consider how to share the day's agenda.

> *Julia*: If there is enough space, I prefer to note key activities and reasons for doing them on the chalkboard and leave this posted. Students can then refer to this agenda whenever they need to orient themselves to the class process. An example of the kinds of things I might write on the board is included in the sample lesson later in this chapter.

If students are just beginning to learn English, it may not be possible to explain the reasons for the tasks, but we can still show them the materials that will be used and the order in which they will be worked on. When students' oral skills are stronger than their written skills, the agenda might be explained orally while one or two key words are recorded on the chalkboard.

Explaining the lesson agenda doesn't mean that we must then stick to it slavishly. Needs that emerge over the course of the lesson may make it clear that changes are necessary. Time considerations can also affect the agenda; misjudging the time needed to complete activities may mean either that we are unable to complete the planned activities or that we finish early and need to add more. When it's necessary to adjust, simply explain what's happening and why.

Once the agenda is shared, it's time to move on to the day's learning tasks, which are discussed later in the chapter.

TAKING A BREAK

Because learning a new language is hard work for both the teacher and students, everyone needs breaks. A good rule is that for every hour of class time, students should have a minimum break of five minutes.

Julia: Because I teach classes that are two hours long, I plan a 10-minute break in the middle of the class. Inevitably, a few students want to use this time to look at their books and study. Because I believe that they will learn more in the rest of the lesson if they have moved around and chatted informally with others, I try to encourage them to do this. Students who are reluctant to take a break are sometimes just shy at first and need encouragement to brave the social scene.

Keep in mind that breaks can be very productive learning time. If there is a lounge where teacher and students can sit together, a great deal of authentic communicative language practice can happen. And, if everyone is participating, this may be a reason for lengthening the break.

In addition, students often choose break-time to approach the teacher about individual needs. While this is fine when quick questions or comments are involved, try to schedule another time for a get-together if the issues are complex. Other students may also wish to speak to us and, furthermore, as teachers, we too need time to ourselves to consider the progress of the lesson or simply to relax.

5. PROVIDING CLOSURE

About 10 minutes before the end of the lesson, it's a good idea to move into the closure phase. At this time, the students can be referred to the agenda to discuss the progress they've made toward their goals. This encourages them to recognize their progress, review key issues and develop an awareness of the needs that are emerging as they progress through the unit. It also gives the teacher an opportunity to assess students' perceptions of the lesson.

6. LOOKING AHEAD

After looking back at the day's session, it's time to look briefly ahead to future lessons. This may include:

— Assigning and discussing homework.
— Talking about the next lesson or future lessons in the current unit.
— Talking about future units.
— Talking about students' needs to use English in their daily lives.

Like closure, looking-ahead involves more than the teacher talking at the students. It's most effective if students are engaged in responding to questions that will help determine the future direction of the course.

This is not the time to carry out detailed planning and needs assessment; it is a time for raising issues, not dealing with them in depth.

Julia: I find the students' comments at looking-ahead time often help me recognize issues that need to be dealt with in more depth. For example, during this phase of one class, a woman raised the issue of car insurance. She was confused by the questions on her renewal form. Her comment sparked other students to acknowledge that they too had trouble dealing with this. As a result, I asked them to bring their car insurance documents to the next class.

During the next lesson, I met with the drivers in the group and used their documents to conduct a needs assessment. This revealed that a number of students were carrying collision insurance on cars barely worth the deductible. When we discussed the needs of these students at the next looking-ahead time, other students identified needs related to other kinds of insurance. Further needs assessment led to the development of a content-based unit on various kinds of insurance.

Although we did not spend a lot of time on the issue during looking-ahead time, this phase of the class provided key opportunities for members of the group to share their needs and sparked an important change in the course.

3. Tasks: The Heart of the Lesson

The tasks students carry out in language classes play a variety of roles in the learning process. While the previous chapters introduced real-world and enabling tasks, the list of tasks can be expanded to include:

— *Assessment tasks*: Include needs assessment and negotiation tasks as well as tasks designed to assess students' learning.
— *Real-world tasks*: The authentic communicative tasks that students wish to carry out successfully in English.
— *Enabling tasks*: Help students develop the skills they need to carry out real-world tasks.
— *Review tasks*: Encourage students to practice skills they have learned in previous lessons.
— *Extension tasks*: Encourage students to apply skills learned in previous lessons in new contexts or for communicative purposes.

When planning lessons, we tailor the tasks to the learning needs of the students. The specific tasks we choose and the order in which they're organized depend on the context and the needs, interests and abilities of the students. As a result, the process is highly variable; there is no single right way to do it every time.

Nevertheless, it's worth keeping the following considerations in mind:

— Enabling tasks are carried out in the context of real-world tasks.
— Tasks build on one another, using skills students developed when completing previous tasks; this limits the new material introduced with a given task and increases opportunities for success.
— Tasks are designed to provide variety in student groupings, content, skills and activities.
— New skills are spiralled; that is, they are introduced, practiced and applied in other communicative contexts.

The sample lesson plan outlined later in this chapter provides a sense of some of the specific ways various tasks can be used to develop lessons.

ORGANIZATIONAL PATTERNS

Although no single blueprint governs the way tasks must be organized within a lesson, many teachers use similar organizational patterns when teaching specific skills—reading, listening, writing and speaking.

Reading

The following procedure works well for tasks designed to develop students' reading comprehension:

Pre-reading:

— To activate their previous knowledge, students think about the topic (e.g., they might work in groups to brainstorm lists of what they already know).
— Students predict the content and organization of the passage using textual features such as pictures and headings.
— Students use their previous knowledge to predict more detailed aspects of content and language.

Reading:

— Students read the passage to find the answers to specific questions relating to the overall idea (e.g., What is the attitude of the writer to her readers? What is the main idea of the reading?).
— Students complete enabling tasks related to the material (e.g., guess word meanings using context clues; find words showing time sequence or cause-and-effect).
— Students complete tasks requiring them to return to the reading and examine it in more detail (e.g., What examples does the writer give of X? What does the writer mean by "barely" in the first paragraph?).

Follow-up:

— Students use the information gained from the reading to complete another task (e.g., Draw a picture of the child the writer describes. Fill in a form with information you learned about the apartment).

Listening

Listening activities can follow much the same pattern as reading. Many of the tasks suggested as examples in the previous section can be used equally well for listening activities.

Pre-listening:

— To activate their previous knowledge, students think about the content of what they will listen to (e.g. if they are going to listen to a conversation about dreams, they might form small groups and, using questions provided by the teacher, discuss their experiences with dreams).
— The teacher outlines the context of what the students are going to hear (e.g., the location and identities of the participants in a conversation).
— Students predict content, vocabulary and structures; if they are going to listen to a news item about an earthquake, invite them to predict words that might be used.

Listening:

— Students listen to complete a manageable communicative task, using language for an authentic purpose.

— Students complete enabling tasks related to the material; this often involves listening to segments of the material again.
— Students listen and complete more complex communicative tasks.

Follow-up:

— Students use the information gained while listening to complete another communicative task (e.g., participating in a class discussion).

Writing

Writing instruction is most effective when students have a clear communicative purpose and an intended audience in mind. The following sequence helps them understand that writing involves a process:

Pre-writing:

— Gather information.
— Plan content and organization.

Writing:

— Write a draft of the composition.

Rewriting:

— Revise the composition, paying attention to content, organization and language.

As the need becomes apparent, enabling tasks may be injected anywhere in this process. For example, if students are writing a letter of complaint to a landlord, organizing a letter may be stressed during the pre-writing phase, and techniques for clarifying time sequence or using modals might be emphasized during the rewriting phase.

Speaking

While there are many effective ways of teaching conversation skills, the following pattern can be adapted to a variety of situations:

— Students hear the language in context (e.g., they listen to a conversation in which an invitation is extended).

— Students clarify the meaning of key words and expressions.
— They practice a range of language needed to fulfill a given purpose (e.g., they repeat segments of the conversation and practice useful alternatives).
— They use the new language in controlled situations (e.g., with a partner, they use pictures to create dialogues inviting the partner to do a range of things).
— They use the new language in less controlled situations (e.g., they role-play conversations that involve inviting their partner to do something).
— They complete a contact task (e.g., outside the classroom, they invite someone to do something).

Each of these steps may involve many tasks designed to work toward the objective in a variety of ways, such as extending, accepting and rejecting invitations, making arrangements relating to time and location, and clarifying details.

Keep in mind that students may encounter a variety of responses when speaking in the real world. For example, many expressions are used to accept or reject invitations. While they may not need to produce the full range of likely responses, students do need to be able to understand them.

Creating Lesson Plans

Although we've used the lesson plan form reproduced on the following page to structure many successful lessons, it is presented here simply as an example. As you gain experience, you will develop a format that suits your own style and the needs of the students you teach.

Nevertheless, we find this particular form useful, if for no other reason than to act as a reminder of the kind of material that it's helpful to include in lesson plans.

Date: Dating lesson plans helps keep them organized.

Unit goals: Although units usually have a number of goals, we usually work toward only one or two in a specific lesson. In this area, we record the unit goal(s) we will be working toward in the particular lesson.

Lesson Plan Form

Date	Resources
Unit Goals	
Lesson Objectives	

Time	Activity	Purpose

Lesson objectives: In this section, we note the specific objectives of the particular lesson. These objectives are usually a more detailed version of the unit goals.

Resources: In this area, we note all the resources, such as tape recorders, video cameras, audio tapes, worksheets and discussion questions, that will be used during the lesson. This enables us to check that everything we need is on hand and reduces the chances of forgetting something.

Activities: This is where we set out both what we will do and what the students will do in carrying out tasks. It also helps to note how students will be grouped and the examples and instructions we will use.

To control the pacing and plan an appropriate amount of material, the *time* each activity is likely to take is noted in a separate column where it can be easily checked. This provides guidance only; most teachers adjust their estimates as the class progresses.

Furthermore, to help maintain focus and ensure that each activity relates to the objectives of the lesson and helps students meet their goals, the *purpose* of each activity is also noted in a separate column. This also enables us to ensure that we have included a balance of activities, emphasizing both practice and application.

A SAMPLE LESSON PLAN

This sample plan for a two-hour session is designed to illustrate how the elements of a specific lesson might be recorded. As a result, it is organized according to the headings shown on the form reproduced on the previous page. Explanatory notes, which would not appear on the lesson plan, are also provided.

When writing lesson plans, it's a good idea to use print that is large enough so that it can be read easily.

Although including the kind of detail outlined in this lesson plan is time-consuming, it is important at first because it helps teachers deliver lessons confidently. As we gain experience, however, many aspects of teaching a lesson become routine and we don't need to spell them out in such detail.

Julia: When I first started teaching, many of my lesson plans were eight to 10 pages long. Because the plans were so detailed, they were hard to use when I was teaching. Although I found that writing out detailed instructions helped me become familiar with teaching routines and feel more confident, I would have been wiser to create a briefer lesson plan and write specific detailed instructions to myself on a separate page.

One way of reducing planning time is to put specific tasks on file cards, which can be re-used when planning lessons for other groups. Although this certainly saves time, be careful about re-using tasks. With a different group of students in a different context, the task as originally planned may not be exactly what is needed. Although I keep records of specific tasks, I find that I use them more often as ideas for developing similar activities than as blueprints for future tasks.

We keep all our lesson plans for a course in a three-ring binder. In addition to lesson plans, the binder also contains copies of materials used in the lessons, as well as class lists, test scores and long-range plans. As a result, it is an important planning resource and helps us demonstrate accountability.

Unit Goals

— Make medical appointment.
— Use hospital emergency services.

Notes: This lesson, part of a topic-based unit on health care, was designed for a group of students who were well along in an introductory ESL course offered in a mid-sized town. The needs assessment process identified making medical appointments and using hospital emergency services as goals for this particular group.

Lesson Objectives

— Asking for an earlier appointment.
— Describing symptoms.
— Knowing when to go to a hospital emergency department.
— Understanding contrast words.

Notes: In the previous lesson, students worked on the language needed to make medical appointments, such as "I'd like to make an appointment," and vocabulary describing health problems, such as "I have a sore leg."

In previous units, students worked on responding to requests for personal information and making and receiving telephone calls. This lesson extends the skills acquired in these units by using them in a new context. From the personal information unit, for example, students will practice giving and spelling their names and using the verb "to be." From the telephone unit, students will practice asking questions, using the future tense, identifying themselves on the phone, ending a phone call, checking understanding, and telling time.

Resources

— Tape player, overhead projector, audio tape of someone making a medical appointment, symptom pictures, copies of reading passage (enough for all students), overhead transparency of title and picture from reading, questions to guide preparation of contrast chart.

Activities

In this section, the entries that would be recorded in the columns designated for time and purpose are shown in square brackets.

Warm-up: Leaving a phone message [7 minutes—review]
Pairs: Students role-play making a phone call and leaving a message. Each student makes and receives a call. Receivers record the message.
Whole group: Students report the messages taken.

Notes: This warm-up reviews telephone language and sets the stage for the activities dealing with using the telephone to make appointments. Notice the authentic outcome—leaving and recording a message. Minimal instruction is needed because it is similar to tasks recently completed in the telephone unit.

When the lesson plan is recorded, the groupings used are highlighted by making them headings for tasks. This enables us to ensure that a variety of groupings is used. It is also an opportunity to think about classroom management issues, such as how to facilitate grouping changes and when to move chairs around.

The agenda: [3 minutes—orient]

Activity	Why?
Make doctor's appointment	Get faster service
Describe health problems	Get better service
Read about using hospitals	Choose when to go

Notes: This shows what would be recorded on the chalkboard. Notice that the language is simpler than that of the lesson objectives, which are for the teacher's use. The reasons given for the activities relate to the way learners are likely to use the skills in their daily lives. The teacher would explain these orally, relating the activities to others completed in earlier lessons. The teacher would also mention particular skills, such as grammar and vocabulary, that will be worked on as part of the activities.

Activity 1: Listen to audio tape of phone call requesting appointment

Pre-listening: [5 minutes—activate previous knowledge]

T: You are sick. You want to go to the doctor. You phone the doctor. What do you say? What questions does the receptionist ask?

Small groups: Students share ideas.

Whole group: Students share group's suggestions.

Notes: This prepares students for the listening task that follows. First, it activates their previous knowledge of making appointments by reviewing material covered in the preceding lesson. Second, it outlines the context of the conversation.

Listening: [10 minutes]

T: Paul is phoning the doctor's office. [establish context] Listen to the tape. What is Paul's problem? When will he go to the doctor? [practice]

Play tape.

Whole group: Students offer answers to teacher's questions.

T: First, the receptionist asks Paul to come on Wednesday. Then she changes the appointment to today. How does Paul get her to change? He does two things. [purpose]

Play tape.

Pairs: Students discuss answers.

T: What words does he use to ask her to change? Write them. [introduce]

Play tape

Same pairs: Students compare written work.
Whole group: Students write answers on chalkboard (e.g., Can I come sooner? It's very painful.). Other students suggest changes and teacher checks.
Listen to tape segment again.
T (pointing to sentences on chalkboard): Here Paul asks to change. Why does he say, "It's very painful"? [purpose]

Notes: Notice that the teacher outlines questions that help students prepare to listen to the taped dialogue. This helps them focus on important information and encourages them to get the big picture. Although the students have not heard this conversation before, this task is manageable because it focuses on aspects of conversation practiced in the previous lesson.

The activities focus not only on the language used but also on the purpose behind the language used, helping students gain information about interactional strategies in their new culture. It also helps emphasize communicative purposes rather than language forms.

Notice also that the students have opportunities to respond to one another's work before the teacher becomes involved, an important aspect of learner-centered classrooms. When students correct another's work, they gain valuable insights into their own learning and confidence in their own skills.

Activity 2: Describing symptoms
Whole group: Brainstorm [10 minutes—introduce]
T: What other reasons can you give for going sooner?
(It's very sore. It's itchy. It's infected. It's swollen. I have a high fever. I feel terrible. I can't sleep.)
Label the list "Symptoms," correct mistakes.
Whole group: Students describe or show meaning of symptoms; as teacher says each, students act out symptoms. [meaning]

Notes: Because the first activity provided a context for the language focused on in this activity, no specific preparation is needed.

Brainstorming elicits language the students already know. Although it's often a good idea to invite students to act as scribes for brainstorming sessions, the teacher is the scribe this time to prevent the pace of the lesson from being slowed by concerns about spelling.

As the students act out the meaning of the expressions, they associate meaning with physical action, a powerful memory tool. An activity such as this can also be a lot of fun, especially if there are a few hams in the group.

Hand out symptom pictures [5 minutes—practice]

Whole group: Students describe the symptoms shown in each picture. Teacher notes changes as needed (e.g., students may need help changing "I" to "he" or "she" or changing verb forms). Students listen and repeat.

Pairs: Students complete dialogue based on the following model by filling in the blank with a symptom from each picture, then change roles [10 minutes—practice]

Receptionist: Can you come on Wednesday at 2:15?
You: Can I come sooner? _____
Receptionist: Okay. How about today at 3:30?

Notes: Notice that most activities are made up of a group of smaller tasks. Some tasks are very short—a matter of a minute or two—whereas others are longer—10 minutes or more.

It's a good idea to leave lots of space on a lesson plan where notes on both the emerging needs of particular students and the effectiveness of the activities can be recorded. After class, this information can be transferred to the appropriate files. If this information isn't noted, it's easily lost or forgotten.

The pictures used for this activity represent a strategy that is frequently used to promote intensive language practice. Like physical activity, visuals help aid memory and encourage students to bypass their first languages. This practice task presents the newly learned vocabulary in the context of a conversation, preparing the students to use the vocabulary to achieve authentic purposes.

Break: [10 minutes]

Activity 3: Phoning for an appointment [15 minutes]
Pairs: Students plan role-play [practice, extend]
Receptionist and sick person. Include problem, request for earlier appointment, symptom.
Students practice role-play and improve it.
Whole group: Pairs perform role-play. [feedback] Audience notes time of appointment, reason for urgency, name of caller.
Teacher gives feedback after all pairs have performed.

Notes: This role-play encourages students to integrate their new skills with the skills acquired in the previous class. They are given roles, a communicative purpose and guidelines setting out specific issues their conversation should touch on. While they have an opportunity to rehearse their conversation, they do not record their parts in writing. When the role-plays are performed for the whole group, the audience is also given a task, which provides extra listening practice. In this instance, the teacher provides feedback on the role-plays to limit the time spent on this activity.

Activity 4: Reading

Pre-reading: [10 minutes—activate previous knowledge]
T: Sometimes we don't go to the doctor's office. We go to the hospital. Why do we go to the hospital?
Small groups: Students think of five good reasons to go to the hospital.
Whole group: Groups report their reasons.
T (showing overhead transparency of title and picture of reading): What do you think the reading is about?
Students suggest ideas.

Notes: Because this activity marks a change in focus, moving the lesson away from making appointments to considering when it's appropriate to use a hospital emergency department, preparation is needed. The pre-reading tasks help do this, as well as activate students' previous knowledge and encourage them to predict the content of the reading.

Reading: Getting the main idea [10 minutes—practice]
T: Read the story and use no more than five words to complete each of these sentences—
You go to Emergency when ....
You go to the doctor's office when ....
Individuals: Read passage and complete sentences.
Small groups: Students compare answers and choose sentences to display on the chalkboard for the whole class.
Whole group: Students discuss similarities and differences in sentences on the chalkboard.

Vocabulary: Words showing contrast [5 minutes—introduce]
Teacher explains what contrast words are and invites students to circle contrast words and expressions in the reading.

Individuals: Read and circle expressions showing contrast.
Whole group: Students report expressions they found as teacher writes them on chalkboard and adds those they may have missed. Students listen and repeat as needed.

Reading: Getting details [10 minutes—practice]
Individuals: Students read passage again and create charts showing specific reasons for going to hospital emergency department or doctor. Teacher collects charts.

Notes: This task begins by focusing students' attention on the main point of the reading. The vocabulary activity is an enabling task that helps them recognize contrasting points, an essential element of this particular passage. After completing it, they are able to identify key considerations in making a decision about whether to go to the emergency department or call their doctor. When reading, students do not need to be able to understand every word; rather, they need to understand only the content that is important to their purpose. This encourages them to read for meaning rather than getting hung up on decoding every unfamiliar word.

Back-Up Activity: Discussion—Comparing Medical Practices
Preparation [10 minutes]
T: What are some ways your country of origin is different from your new country? [generate content]
Whole group: As students respond, teacher records information on chalkboard under headings "Different" and "Same."
Teacher uses information to model using expressions showing similarities (e.g., "both," "too," "like") and differences (e.g., "but," "however," "unlike"). [review, introduce]
Students use expressions to talk about other similarities and differences.

Discussion: [15 minutes—practice]
Small groups: Four or five students from different home cultures discuss a series of prepared questions on medical practices. Teacher goes over the questions to check students' comprehension and appoints a scribe for each group to note interesting similarities and differences to report to the class. As groups discuss, teacher circulates and notes issues for later discussion, especially use of expressions showing similarities and differences.

Follow-up: [5 minutes—feedback]
Whole group: Scribes report a few interesting similarities and differences. Teacher gives feedback on language use.

Notes: When planning a lesson, it's important to keep a back-up activity in reserve. Sometimes, the planned activities take less time than expected. At other times, something goes wrong—a guest speaker doesn't show up or a piece of equipment breaks down. At still other times, some of the planned activities seem inappropriate for the energy level or mood of the class. A back-up activity enables the teacher to deal with these situations confidently.

> *Julia*: I got caught without a back-up during the first lesson I ever taught. I thought I was prepared, but the students whipped right through the planned activities and, because of my inexperience, I didn't yet have the tools to extend and enrich them. As a result, halfway through the two-hour lesson, I found myself with no idea of what to do next. I announced the break, quaking in my boots about what the next hour would bring. The need of the moment, of course, forced me to think of something and, as I recall, it didn't turn out too badly, but that day I decided I would never again be caught without plenty of back-up.
>
> If back-up activities aren't used, planning them isn't a waste of time because they can often become part of subsequent lessons. I often have two back-ups in reserve. Because one is an activity I know I will use in the next lesson, it's really part of the planning for that lesson. The other, usually something fun, is often suited to a variety of situations and designed to contribute to students' overall language development. This kind of activity is especially useful when there is a need to lighten the class. It might be a game, a song, or a jazz chant (see Carolyn Graham's book *Jazz Chants* in "Additional Reading").

The suggested back-up activity is a good follow-up to the reading activity because it gives students an opportunity to use information gained from the reading as well as terms that express contrast. It could also be used in the following lesson. If it is recorded on a separate page, it can be transferred easily to the next lesson.

It also helps students consolidate their understanding of medical practices in their new country and practice explaining how things are done in their country of origin, something immigrants often want to do in social situations. Recognizing the variety of medical practices around the world also helps students accept that there are often many different ways of doing things. Examining how cultures differ helps them view practices not as right or wrong, but simply as different.

Closure: [5 minutes—review, assess]
> T: What activities did we do today? In the conversation activity, what did we practice? What new words did you learn? In the reading, did any information surprise you? What are some words we use to show difference? Do you have any questions or comments about today's class?

Notes: Noting this part of the plan in question form encourages us to elicit information from students rather than pontificating on what the class has done. The students know best what new skills and insights they have developed over the course of the lesson. Furthermore, engaging students in revisiting aspects of the day's lesson helps them review the material and recognize their accomplishments.

Looking ahead: [5 minutes]
> Homework: [practice] Get a partner. Plan a time to phone each other. Do appointment role-plays over the phone. For the next class, be prepared to tell about your role-plays.
> *Whole group*: [assess] Students report communication experiences since last class.
> Next time: [prepare] Going to Emergency—video
> Making an appointment for someone else.

Notes: In this lesson, looking-ahead time has three components. First, homework is assigned—in this case, a follow-up to the role-play completed in class. Because ESL students are sometimes intimidated at the prospect of talking on the telephone, inviting them to practice this with a fellow student helps build their confidence as they practice their new skills.

Next, students report on their communication experiences outside the classroom. Although in some ways this represents looking back rather than ahead, it provides information about the needs students are experiencing in their daily lives. This information can be used when planning future lessons or units. Finally, the teacher offers some information about the plans for the next lesson, providing students with an opportunity to respond while there is still time to make changes.

Conclusion

When planning effective lessons, we must consider various factors affecting students' learning. These include the role of the lesson in helping achieve the goals of the unit and the course, as well as the comfort of the students. We need to provide enough variety so that we don't bore them, at the same time as we ensure that there are enough familiar tasks and procedures so that they are not confused. Our lessons must also provide students with plenty of opportunity to practice and integrate newly learned skills when fulfilling authentic communicative purposes.

Furthermore, we must consider various aspects of tasks in relation to one another. These include the grouping of the students, the variety of tasks and skills, and the building of both skills and positive attitudes toward language-learning and themselves as language learners.

Although it's important to consider these factors at the lesson-planning stage, many of them also affect the choices we make when putting our plans into practice. The next chapter focuses on what happens at this stage.

. . . .

PUTTING PLANS
INTO ACTION

No matter how carefully we plan units, lessons and tasks, the moment of truth arrives when we enter the classroom ready to put our plans into action. It is at this stage that our planning ability must be integrated with a variety of other skills that are essential to ensuring that students have an opportunity to become interested, motivated, successful learners.

Because our goal is to work with the learners to create the physical, psychological and interpersonal conditions that will enable them to become effective learners, we need to be aware of the classroom dynamics and the actions and attitudes that support adult learning, both inside and outside the classroom. Furthermore, we need to recognize the kinds of problems that can arise in adult ESL classes so that we can develop creative ways of solving them.

Managing the Classroom

CREATING A SUPPORTIVE LEARNING CLIMATE

People learn best in a warm, supportive atmosphere where they feel comfortable about participating. Teachers can help create this kind of "safe" environment by fostering positive relationships with—and among—students and by paying attention to the physical arrangements in the class.

Fostering Positive Relationships

A vital first step toward recognizing students' individuality and their importance to the group is to learn their names. Occasionally, native English-speakers are tempted to take the easy way out by Anglicizing names. We advise against this. Accepting and using the students' names is a sign of respect. A rare exception may occur when a name sounds offensive in English, but this should be discussed first with the student.

Because naming systems differ among cultures, the best bet is to ask students what they wish to be called—and tell them what we want them to call us. Although students call teachers by their first names in many adult classes, some students may feel this is disrespectful. If students aren't comfortable using your first name, don't force the issue.

It's also important to help students learn names and get to know one another. Here are some strategies for doing this:

— Play a memory game by inviting students to speak in this pattern:
  Student 1: My name is ....
  Student 2: His (her) name is .... My name is ....
  Student 3: Their names are ... and .... My name is ....
  Students add their own names in turn until the last person says everyone's name. A cheer often goes up when this happens.
— Working in pairs, students introduce their partners to the rest of the class.
— Invite students to ask questions of others, prefixing each question with the student's name.
— Encourage students to talk about their culture and experiences with one another (e.g., tell about the school you went to, your first job, your family, etc.).

Many other strategies also help students feel welcome and comfortable. For example, greeting them by name as they arrive in class sends the message that their presence is valued and that we are interested in each of them.

It's also important to acknowledge—and welcome—students' contributions to class activities. Even when their responses don't seem appropriate, we can encourage them to stay engaged and keep trying by asking questions such as, "Were you thinking of...?"

Students should never feel put down. Participation dries up when they feel that they have taken a risk and failed. When corrections are necessary, we can emphasize the positive by drawing attention to what they did well and encouraging them to work with us to make improvements where necessary. We can also introduce techniques for making criticism less personal. For example, several students might write sentences on the chalkboard, then sit down. This helps place the emphasis of the subsequent discussion on the sentences rather than on the students who wrote them.

When giving positive feedback, be careful not to patronize students by overpraising. An encouraging nod is often enough to let them know they're on track.

Students' strengths, interests and talents are an important resource in any classroom. For example, a student who is skilled with audio-visual equipment might take responsibility for operating it. By searching out and showing respect for students' non-linguistic abilities, we recognize—and remind them of—what they *can* do. This bolsters their confidence as they work on learning English.

Adult students respond well when teachers genuinely share who they are and what they feel. Of course, this doesn't mean that it's appropriate to use students as therapy substitutes; this would be an abuse of our responsibility. It does mean, however, being honest with them. For example, when we don't know the answer to a question, we have a terrific opportunity to model the process of finding out the answer. By doing so, we present ourselves as fellow learners and foster the idea that we are involved in a learning partnership with the students.

One of the most important things teachers can do is demonstrate our belief that the students can—and want to—learn. Once we have prepared them by giving clear instructions, we must trust them to get on with the task. Be available to give assistance but leave the ball in their court. If a task is too difficult, simplify or shorten it; help them experience success by completing a more limited task.

When differences arise over issues such as how people learn language, it's important to remember that we all have culturally bound views of appropriate educational methodologies. Assume that the students' perspectives are appropriate in their home cultures. Like our own ideas, theirs are a product of their life experience, culture and education. Because we can't expect students to embrace new ways of doing things immediately, it helps to introduce new techniques gradually.

Some students are used to learning by rote, which often involves memorizing and rehearsing lessons in preparation for class.

> *Mary*: When I asked a group of students to come to class prepared to tell folktales from their native countries, one student wrote out and memorized a long story about a princess. While she no doubt learned something from doing this, her delivery was difficult to understand because she was concentrating on retrieving language rather than expressing it. In retrospect, I realize that once this student had recited her story, it would have been a good idea to encourage her to practice speaking spontaneously by inviting the group to ask her questions (e.g., Who was the story about? Where did it take place? What happened? Why did the princess…? How did she…?).

While it doesn't hurt to invite students to memorize occasionally, we need to focus on designing tasks that encourage them to use natural speech for communicative purposes and create meaning on the spot. This kind of practice helps them build the confidence they need to begin interacting in English outside the classroom.

Laughter is a wonderful tool for releasing tension and establishing the kind of relaxed learning climate in which students feel free to participate actively. Learning and fun make good partners. Pointing out life's incongruities often sparks laughter and encourages students to do the same. Of course, humor must be combined with sensitivity. There is no humor when students feel put down.

Groupwork, an important element of learner-centered approaches, provides a variety of benefits. Students inevitably participate more actively and, therefore, use more English. They get to know their fellow students and feel freer to express themselves as they learn language from one another. They also learn about other cultures and make new friends. Specific techniques for successfully introducing groupwork are discussed more extensively later in this chapter.

Creating a Comfortable Physical Setting

Because everyone tends to be more relaxed and comfortable in a pleasant setting, part of the teacher's role is to ensure that the physical arrangements of the classroom contribute to a positive learning environment. This means that we must be alert to conditions that may interfere with learning. For example, are students having trouble seeing the chalkboard or is the sun in their eyes?

Keep in mind that adults generally need brighter lights and warmer rooms than younger people. Shivering through a two-hour class isn't likely to enhance learning.

Ideally, seating should be flexible so that the layout can be altered to suit different tasks. For example, when the teacher is the focus of attention—during activities involving the whole class, for example—a horseshoe arrangement works well because the students can see the teacher and each other. This arrangement promotes free-flowing interaction.

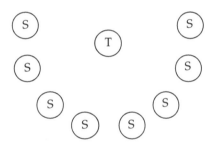

When students are working in pairs or small groups, it helps if they can move their chairs close to each other. Keep in mind, however, that it isn't always practical to shift furniture. When students are working in pairs only briefly or returning to the whole group for just a few minutes, moving all the chairs simply isn't worth it. Incidentally, ask students to do the rearranging. This helps get them involved and fosters the feeling that it's their classroom.

When the physical conditions are less than satisfactory, it may be necessary to exercise creativity. Start by trying to find alternative accommodations. For example, adult ESL classes are occasionally scheduled in classrooms designed for children. Because sitting in a child-sized chair for any length of time can be very uncomfortable—as well as demeaning—it's important to push administrators to rectify the situation.

Mary: I once visited an ESL class in which the students sat for three hours on lab stools. By the third hour, many of them were more focused on trying to get comfortable than on learning English. Try sitting in the students' chairs for an extended period yourself to check them out.

If finding alternative accommodations isn't possible, try to find other solutions. For example, if the room is too cool, discuss the problem with the students and figure out ways of compensating, such as wearing heavier clothing, scheduling short exercise periods, or leaving the lights on when the room is vacant.

Julia: On one occasion, I taught a class assigned to a room with a leaky ceiling. To cope, we changed the seating arrangements, used the lounge when it was available, and complained to the administration. Although the problem wasn't resolved immediately, we managed to continue the class and got a better room eventually.

USING EQUIPMENT EFFECTIVELY

Using classroom equipment effectively helps students learn. Nevertheless, we're all familiar with the kinds of things that can go wrong when we're relying on audio-visual equipment to help with lessons. To avoid last-minute surprises, check in advance to ensure that the equipment is in working order. Use good-quality audio or videotapes and set them up ahead of time so that they're ready to play when needed. As they're playing, check to make sure the volume is at a comfortable level.

Although the chalkboard is often taken for granted, it's an important piece of classroom equipment that contributes to learning when it's used effectively. Start by making sure there is an adequate supply of chalk and brushes. Our writing is a model for the students; make sure it's legible and large enough for everyone to read. Don't mix printing and writing or upper and lower case letters. Keep in mind that it may be necessary to print when students aren't experienced at reading cursive script. And start on the left and keep the writing organized so students can follow.

While the chalkboard can be very useful, try not to write on it too much. And avoid writing on the board and talking at the same time. Students may have trouble hearing clearly, and sometimes try to copy rather than listen. If copying is necessary, assure them that they will have time to do so later—then be sure to follow up on this promise.

WORKING IN GROUPS

While encouraging students to work in groups is an effective, learner-centered strategy, it requires planning and preparation, as well as careful monitoring of the process and the outcomes.

Working in groups has many benefits:

— It promotes intensive language practice by enabling more than one person to speak at a time. There are as many speakers as there are groups.
— It encourages students to take responsibility for their own learning.
— It helps learners relate to and learn from one another.
— It helps build cooperative relationships.
— It can help change interaction patterns.
— It encourages learners to change position and move around the room.

Like any technique, however, grouping can be overused. We suggest maintaining a balance of individual, whole-class and small-group activities.

Groups can be established for a variety of purposes and their composition may vary depending on the task and the social dynamics at work in the class. For example, if students often rely on their first language, it may be a good idea to assign those who speak the same language to different groups.

For some tasks, heterogeneous groups are a good idea; for others, homogeneous groups may make more sense. Students may be grouped on the basis of their first languages, ages, sexes, language levels or interests.

The size of groups also varies according to the purpose of the task. For example, tasks involving intensive practice are usually carried out most effectively in pairs while problem-solving and discussion tasks work well with groups of three or four.

Groupwork is most effective when the purpose and expected outcomes of the activity are clear. Students need to understand what they are supposed to do, what product is expected, and what they will learn by completing the task.

On occasion, it's a good idea to arrange for student observers to note and comment on elements of the group process, such as interaction patterns relating to, for example, the number of times each member spoke or the way the group reached decisions.

Sometimes, a group member may be responsible for presenting the group's work to the class. This may involve reporting the solution to a problem or the results of a discussion of an issue. Assigning a reporter helps the group focus on the task at hand and recognizes the group's accomplishment.

When setting up tasks for small groups, it's a good idea to give the instructions to the whole class before rearranging seating or structuring the groups. This ensures that the students' attention isn't distracted.

Give clear instructions and indicate how much time is available so students can pace themselves. Although tasks may take anywhere from five minutes to half an hour, students who are just beginning to learn English may not be able to sustain an activity for more than five or 10 minutes.

Prepare handouts ahead of time and have them ready to give out. Giving only one copy to each group requires students to share the information or instructions and reduces the likelihood that they will try to complete the task individually.

Once group activities are complete, a debriefing session is often useful. At this time, the teacher can invite students to comment on the task, the process and the outcomes. When appropriate, it's also a good idea to display the products of the group activities or review them with the class as a whole. If there isn't time to comment in detail on every group's efforts, focus on a particular aspect of each group's work or invite each to report one idea.

WORKING WITH MULTI-LEVEL CLASSES

Although no class is ever entirely homogeneous, the range of proficiency in English is far wider in some classes than in others. When a class includes students whose skills are dramatcially different, the teacher faces a unique—but not insurmountable—challenge. In fact, a number of strategies can help make the learning experience successful for everyone. Although some of these are introduced here, Jill Bell offers a *Source* much more detailed look at the subject in her book, *Teaching* ✗ *Multilevel Classes in ESL* (see "Additional Reading").

If the needs assessment indicates, for example, that making plans for social events is of interest to the whole group, the class may be divided into smaller homogeneous groups based on the students' proficiency in English. Tasks relating to the overall theme can then be tailored to the proficiency level of each group. A lesson dealing with making plans to go to a movie with friends might include the following tasks:

— *Groups whose English skills are limited*: Read movie ads, choose one and decide what time to go; identify the phone number to call for more information; look up the address of the theater in the listings or phone book.
— *Groups whose English skills are more advanced*: Read movie descriptions and select one; decide where and when to meet.
— *Groups whose English skills are the most advanced*: Read and criticize movie reviews; decide which movie to see; find out where it's playing; call for information about matinees and admission prices.

When teaching a multi-level class, it's important to make an effort to develop rapport within the group as a whole. One way of doing this is to plan whole-group activities, including debriefings after small-group sessions.

Another strategy involves pairing a student whose English skills are fairly advanced with another whose skills are less proficient and giving the two a cooperative assignment. For instance, if the students are to plan the refreshments for an event, the less proficient English-speaker might have information about how many people will be present and the money available. The more proficient speaker might have a price list and information on the guests' food and drink preferences. To come up with a menu, they must share this information.

This strategy encourages students to contribute based on their proficiency. Although more proficient students can learn a great deal from activities such as this, some may not appreciate their benefits. As a result, this technique should be used carefully.

Some adult ESL classes include students who have few or no literacy skills in their first language. Sometimes this is because they have had little or no formal education in their first language; at others, it's because their language doesn't have a written form.

These students can't be expected to cope with printed or written material of any kind. They need individualized help from both the teacher and the other students. When possible, it helps to enlist a teacher's aide or an outside volunteer, preferably one who speaks the student's language. Take time to give the volunteer guidance about what the class is doing and how to work with the student. Materials, such as cards for teaching sight words and literacy workbooks, can be helpful, although the volunteer should use these selectively. Literacy students typically make slow progress and require more attention than literate students.

MANAGING TIME

In the previous chapter, we suggested estimating and noting the time needed to complete each phase of a lesson. As the lesson progresses, it may be necessary to adjust the estimates, adding or subtracting time, or paring down tasks.

Individuals and groups rarely finish tasks at exactly the same time. When a group rushes through a task, check the results and show them how they could get more out of it.

On the other hand, if a group finishes well ahead of other groups and has done a thorough job, there are several options:

— Provide enrichment tasks prepared for just such a situation. These might include an extension of the task, such as adding another discussion question or another problem to be solved.
— Invite the group to chart the results of a discussion task or create a flow chart showing the problem-solving process it used.
— Suggest that the group prepare a chart on which the task results can be entered as other groups finish. This will enable them to compare findings.

Sometimes, one group takes much longer to finish a task than others. When this happens, it may be necessary to ask this group to present a progress report rather than completing the task. If finishing is important to prepare for subsequent tasks, suggest that the group meet after class or allot time during the next class.

When individual students finish early, it helps to have resources, such as audio tapes with headphones or reading materials, ready for them to use. They might also work on their journals or help students who have not yet finished.

DEALING WITH INDIVIDUAL NEEDS

Although teachers must be prepared to take into account the needs, interests and abilities of individual learners, it is impractical to introduce an individual program for every student. Nevertheless, it is often possible to address many individual needs within the context of an overall theme. For example, a student who is having trouble learning might be invited to take home tapes of role-plays created in class and asked to record expressions that were central to the lesson.

A student who is not interested in a theme that is popular with other students might be invited to complete an alternative task that uses similar language skills. For example, if the class is working on understanding paychecks, a student who is not expecting to join the workforce might be invited to deal with other forms of abbreviated print information, such as that found on utility bills.

Every class includes students with a variety of preferred learning styles. Some people learn more efficiently with the support of visuals, while others respond to oral presentations. Some benefit from physical involvement, such as carrying out particular actions, while still others learn through tactile experiences such as handling letters or tracing them with a finger. To ensure that students have opportunities to learn in ways that are most comfortable, plan a variety of tasks that call on them to use a variety of senses.

While it's certainly possible to meet individual needs, doing so is demanding. To avoid stretching yourself too thin, keep in mind that a teacher's first priority is the good of the class; the importance of meeting individual needs must be weighed against the demands this makes on our time, energy and ability.

In most cases, teachers are expected to keep attendance records. Rather than calling the roll in adult classes, we suggest simply noting who is absent. Many institutions also require teachers to keep a record of test scores to demonstrate accountability.

In addition to these institutional requirements, however, experienced teachers also keep a variety of other records that help when planning. As suggested in the previous chapter, these include notes on students' special capabilities and needs, as well as on aspects of language that need more work.

Many teachers also keep samples of students' work over time in order to provide a concrete record of their progress. Records like these can be used to draw students' attention to their developing English skills. Language-learning is a long process and concrete reminders of the progress they have made help build students' morale and prevent them from becoming discouraged.

> *Mary*: As a program coordinator visiting a class, I was impressed when a student showed me her notebook with great pride. She pointed out the way she had written when she first joined the class, then flipped to her current work to show me how much she had improved. This student was maintaining her own record of progress.

Communicating with Students

The teacher's ability to communicate effectively is a key ingredient of successful ESL programs.

OVERCOMING THE LANGUAGE BARRIER

Working with students who are just beginning to learn English calls for ingenuity. One of the most important suggestions we can make is to use English to teach English. If the teacher speaks the students' first language and uses it to communicate, students may come to depend on this. Furthermore, in this situation, students are more likely to continue translating from their first language, rather than learning to think in English. While there will be times when a quick translation helps everyone over a hump, these occasions should be the exception rather than the rule.

Be aware that native English-speakers sometimes unconsciously equate lack of language with deafness and shout in effort to make themselves understood. Try to speak in a normal voice, being careful not to overpronounce words or use unnatural stress and intonation. This helps prepare students to understand the language they will hear in the community.

At the same time, when teaching a particular structure, it's a good idea to model it carefully so that students are able hear all the sounds. For example, in the sentence "I'd like to swim," students may not hear the *d* in "I'd" if the teacher speaks normally. Because the difference between "I like to swim," and "I'd like to swim," is significant, slowing down and overstressing the *d* is important to ensure that students hear it. Once the point is made, however, we can return to speaking normally and encourage students to do the same.

It helps to use concrete objects and visuals, such as pictures, charts, photographs, diagrams, graphs and drawings, to get across meaning. Demonstrating actions is also useful, especially when explaining the meanings of verbs and adjectives, such as "ambled" and "huge." This also helps create interest, variety and humor.

MANAGING TEACHER TALK

Because the students are the ones who need to practice speaking, it's important for teachers to limit how much we speak. We suggest that teacher talk be used primarily to give instructions and explanations, elicit comments from the students, model language, and provide support and feedback.

Using hand signals to impart frequently used instructions is one way of reducing the amount of teacher talk. For example, to indicate that it's time for students to listen, we might cup an ear with our hand.

After the teacher models a language item, it's a good idea to rely on the students who caught it the first time to model it for the others. If the teacher says it over and over, students may not listen as attentively. By limiting our own modeling, we help learners improve their listening skills.

When giving instructions, keep them simple and ensure that they apply to only one task at a time. Think them through before the class and give students a chance to ask for clarification. We can't assume that students understand us. To check their comprehension, it's a good idea to ask students to restate instructions. The teacher or a student can also list the steps on the chalkboard or a handout can be prepared for reference. Simply asking students if they understand is often futile. People tend to say yes, whether they mean it or not.

USING QUESTIONS EFFECTIVELY

Because responding to questions provides students with opportunities to practice using English, it's important to design questions that enhance these opportunities.

Types of Questions

Essentially, there are two kinds of questions: display questions and communicative questions.

Display questions are those to which the teacher already knows the answers. While the answers don't provide any new information, they may be used to practice a grammatical form or vocabulary. For example, pointing to an apple, the teacher might ask, "What's this?" Answering this questions gives students an opportunity to practice using the structure, "It's an...."

Display questions are also used to check students' comprehension. For example, after a reading, the teacher might ask, "Who were the main characters? Were they friends?"

While display questions can be useful, we recommend limiting their use because they have little communicative value and are low in interest.

Communicative questions are asked in real interactions between people, usually to elicit the information needed to fill in an information gap (e.g., What's your phone number? What do you think of the public transit system?). They promote real communication, especially when the information exchanged is of value or interest.

Response Time

When asking questions of adult ESL students, teachers need to be aware of the importance of response time. Silence is not stressful to the learner who knows the answer and is formulating a response. Don't jump in too soon and answer the question for the student. If a student is unable to answer, move on to another. When someone gives the answer, return to the first student to give her another go at it.

It also helps to teach students what to say when they don't know an answer. "I don't know" and "I don't understand" are handy responses in any circumstances. Furthermore, in Western cultures, they are accepted more readily than silence.

Students' Questions

In addition to answering questions, it's important for students to have as many opportunities as possible to ask questions. Generating the language needed to do so increases their self-reliance.

One effective strategy is to invite students to work in pairs, asking each other questions. For example, if students bring pictures of relatives to class during a unit on the family, they can pair up and ask each other questions about the pictures, such as, "Is he your father?" "Is she your aunt?" and "What does he do?"

Another popular technique is to invite a visitor—another teacher, an advanced student from another class, someone from the community—to the class to answer students' questions. It works best if these questions are brainstormed in advance, but it isn't a good idea for the students to read them. For a work-related unit, for example, the visitor selected might be a job counselor or someone who has recently found a job. The students' questions might focus on finding out about the person's experience in job interviews—"What did they ask you?" "What did you wear?"

Providing Effective Feedback

Students benefit from feedback that focuses both on what they do well and what they need to improve. When they give correct or interesting answers, or when they have overcome a language problem, acknowledge their success. The teacher's response need only be sincere, not elaborate. The emphasis should be on noticing what's right.

In most cases, students expect—and want—the teacher to correct their errors. Making errors is part of language-learning, and students learn from their mistakes—when they get appropriate feedback. However, it's important to use judgment about correcting errors. Be selective. Consider the goals of the activity. Is the focus on fluency or accuracy?

If the goal is to improve accuracy, ask yourself the following questions before making a correction:

— Does the mistake represent an error in the form being taught? If it does, make a correction. If not, simply note it for future attention.
— Does the mistake represent an oral slip or a real error? Native speakers make slips too. If it is a slip, ignore it.
— Can the student correct his own error? Try it and find out.
— Does the error point to a problem that calls for more focused attention? If so, it may be necessary to plan an activity designed to clear up the problem.

If the goal is to improve fluency, on the other hand, it helps to ask yourself the following questions before correcting:

— Will stopping the student interrupt a natural flow of extemporaneous speech? In the uncontrolled parts of a lesson, students should feel free to experiment with applying what they have learned. If the teacher interrupts constantly, the flow of speech will dry up. When a student has finished speaking, the teacher can identify selected errors for the group to correct.
— Does the error affect communication? If the learner can't be understood, it may be necessary to correct. However, students also need opportunities to practice overcoming communication breakdowns themselves. Intervene only if students are unable to resolve the problem.

Some errors are, in fact, signs of progress. For example, when students add *ed* to all past tense verbs, it's clear that they have internalized the *ed* rule. The next step is to introduce the irregular verbs (e.g., "go," "come," "break" and "have") as they arise in context.

A variety of strategies can be used effectively to correct errors in speaking and writing:

— If students are likely to know the correct form, just signal that something is awry. They may correct themselves. For a speaking error, a tilt of the head or a slightly quizzical expression makes an effective signal.

For writing errors, a question mark in the margin is often all that's needed.
— Put the incorrect sentence on the board and ask students to suggest ways of improving it.
— If the error represents one individual's ingrained habit, make a note of it and plan some intensive practice for the student. We don't recommend drilling the whole class when only one student is having trouble with a particular point.

Keep in mind that a single correction doesn't ensure that a student will get something right forever after. To integrate the correct form, students need to practice it in several short sessions with breaks in between.

It isn't unusual for students to make many errors when they write. The teacher can't—and shouldn't—correct everything. It helps to start by checking on meaning. Make an effort to find out what the student was trying to say and help her get it on paper. Once the meaning is clear, we can start to deal with selected aspects of usage, grammar and vocabulary.

Perfection is not the goal. Students learn more effectively when we focus on correcting certain items. When selecting these items, we must consider both the student's level of proficiency and how basic to overall language development the error is.

Pronunciation, grammar and word-order errors often occur when students transfer to English rules from their first languages. For example, some languages do not indicate plurals by adding affixes. As a result, a Cantonese-speaker is likely to translate "two oranges" as "two orange." Don't get hung up on errors like this. This feature of English has low communicative value and is, in any case, redundant; the number "two" makes the s unnecessary for understanding.

While making mistakes is part of the learning process, it's important not to overdo corrections to the point where learners become embarrassed, frustrated and uncomfortable. Stop before this happens. Make a note of the problem and return to it another day. Studies have shown that the students' comfort influences their ability to learn language successfully.

Dealing With Problems

Because adult learners are usually well-motivated, attentive and enjoy the fellowship of other students, teaching them is very rewarding. Nevertheless, problems can—and do—arise.

INTERPERSONAL ISSUES

Students may encounter problems stemming from interpersonal issues. When this happens, we need to consider the source of the difficulty. Is the course addressing a particular student's needs? Are issues that go beyond the classroom influencing the student's performance? While we can't necessarily solve the underlying problems, reflecting on them can expand our insights and help us develop strategies designed to encourage the student to learn.

Participation

Students who are inattentive or reluctant to participate often respond well in small-group sessions, especially if they are appointed the group's scribe or reporter. This helps them feel engaged and builds their confidence, preparing them to take a more active part in whole-class activities.

Focusing on a student's talent or area of expertise by casting him in the role of expert and inviting other students to ask questions is another strategy that works well. Sometimes, simply drawing special attention to a piece of work provides a boost. Often, small successes are all that's needed to bolster confidence and increase participation.

While most students understand that the teacher's time must be shared, we occasionally encounter learners who place excessive demands on us. When this happens, we need to be clear about what is reasonable. A student who hands in reams of writing and expects it to be corrected, for example, must be told that time constraints make this impossible. Try asking the student to write half a page instead, or focus her efforts by referring her to independent study materials.

Finally, here are some strategies to try with students who monopolize the class:

— Encourage other students to participate by calling on them specifically.

- When forming groups, place assertive students to-gether.
- Explain that others, too, must have a chance to speak.
- Recognize these students' strengths.
- Ask demanding students to help others with specific language issues.
- Suggest that demanding students act as observers or reporters.

If all else fails, it may be necessary to explain privately that others, too, need opportunities to participate. Then, discuss ways of taking part more appropriately.

Student-Student Relations

In a class that includes students from a variety of back-grounds, relations can sometimes become strained, especially when negative stereotypes prevalent in learners' home cultures are transferred to their new environment. Although these are often mitigated as individuals get to know each other and participate in cooperative activities, harmony isn't always achieved painlessly. At times, it may be necessary for the teacher to step in to defuse friction.

In some cases, introducing awareness-raising activities is all that's needed. Often, this simply involves examining behavior that is considered appropriate in English-speaking cultures. Ideas for topics and suitable classroom activities are sometimes suggested in ESL textbooks.

If the subtle approach doesn't bring about changes in students' attitudes and behavior, try talking to the individual student(s) about appropriate ways of acting. Sometimes, it may be necessary to reduce the potential for friction by changing the way students are grouped.

Student-Teacher Relations

Inevitably, some students look to the teacher for help with personal problems. When this happens, it's important to focus on our role as teacher. Our responsibility is to lend a sympathetic ear and, if appropriate, refer the student to a professional, such as the institution's counselor, or a multicultural or medical agency. If we become immersed in students' personal problems, we may have trouble fulfilling our teaching responsibilities and the class can suffer as a result. Furthermore, without specialized training, we may end up doing more harm than good.

When dealing with a diverse group of adults, it's important to remember that much of human behavior—including our own—is deeply rooted in cultural norms instilled from birth. As teachers, we must be particularly sensitive to this, especially when students behave in ways that might be considered inappropriate from our point of view. Occasionally, we may even find ourselves becoming irritated by behavior that may be considered acceptable, even encouraged, in a student's home culture. When this happens, we need to acknowledge—and reflect on—our feelings, remembering that our own reactions are as culturally bound as the behavior that sparked them. If we expect students to accept features of their new culture that they find strange and work harmoniously and respectfully with people from a variety of backgrounds, then we must be prepared to do the same. Our own behavior is a model for the students and, as we help them grow and develop an awareness of the impact of ingrained cultural attitudes, we are also helping ourselves.

ATTENDANCE AND PUNCTUALITY

Adult learners have adult responsibilities at home and at work that sometimes prevent them from attending class regularly. And because many of them carry heavy loads, they may occasionally be too tired to be attentive even when they are present. Asking those who can't attend to phone ahead to let us know they'll be absent helps us focus on the students who are in class.

In addition, it isn't unusual to encounter students with different attitudes about the value of punctuality. Sometimes, these differences are the result of cultural influences. Because punctuality is valued in Western society—we expect people to be on time for work, school, appointments and social engagements—it's important for us to set an example by:

— Being at class early, ready to start on time.
— Beginning the lesson with a warm-up activity. If punctuality is a problem, the warm-up can delay the introduction of the main tasks of the lesson until everyone has arrived.

116

— Keeping the pace going as latecomers arrive and involving them as soon as they get settled.
— Discussing cultural customs related to time. Do this after latecomers arrive. Don't rail at those who were on time!

Encouraging Students to Learn outside the Classroom

A variety of strategies can be used to encourage students to work on improving their English skills outside the class.

HOMEWORK ASSIGNMENTS

When selecting a homework assignment, we must consider the benefits. Does it reinforce what the students have worked on in class? Does it extend their learning? Does it foster the use of independent learning strategies?

Homework can involve formal pencil-and-paper tasks such as writing a journal entry on a specific topic or reading assignments. It can also involve something like listening to and reporting on a news item, or a community contact task, such as initiating an interaction with a sales clerk. Whatever the assignment, it should be within students' capabilities, relate to what they have been learning in class, and followed up on in the next class.

Keep in mind that when we assign written work, we must be prepared to provide feedback that will help students learn. Simply marking something wrong or correcting it with no explanation is worthless. A short assignment covered in depth is more worthwhile than expecting students to complete pages of material that will never be looked at again.

While some students are eager for homework, others may consistently fail to complete assignments. When this happens, we must consider why. Are the assignments too long, too hard, too easy or too numerous? Are the instructions clear? Is feedback given promptly so that students realize that their efforts are valued?

Furthermore, we must recognize that some students simply have little time for homework because they are already overwhelmed by work and family responsibilities.

Taking responsibility for their own learning may be an unfamiliar concept to students educated in school systems that focused on the teacher as the transmitter of all knowledge. As a result, they may need help to understand that they can become independent learners.

Using the Community

It's important to help students identify opportunities for both practicing English outside the classroom and using the community as a resource for learning. In some cases, this may simply involve discussing strategies they can use to improve their English skills on their own. In others, it may mean assigning specific tasks designed to encourage them to use resources outside the classroom. For example, we can invite students to ask for something in a store or office and bring it to class, or listen to other people's interactions on the bus, in lineups and in stores and collect new expressions.

We can also encourage them to use community resources by planning a field trip to a community center or library. Getting involved in volunteer work and recreational activities is a good way to meet native speakers and use English.

In the workplace, many students tend to stick with people who speak their home language, a natural reaction when so many things are new and strange. Nevertheless, the workplace provides many opportunities for learning English; we can help students build bridges to English-speakers by working on conversation openers and appropriate subjects for the kind of small talk that goes on at coffee breaks.

Some institutions have introduced language-partner programs, which involve matching ESL students with English-speaking conversation partners for a specified period every week. The institution usually provides the English-speakers with the training necessary to do this effectively.

Using the Media

While newspapers, radio and television are important resources, students may need help to learn to use them effectively. Understanding the underlying framework of broadcast news reports and print stories helps them anticipate what is coming and realize that the same information is often presented in different ways. Getting the gist is important; encourage them not to give up because they don't understand some of the words. The news is a good resource because students can listen for repeat broadcasts of the same items and follow the development of an item over several days. Newspaper reports reinforce information that is broadcast on radio and TV and vice versa.

While news reports may be too difficult for those who are just beginning to learn English, ads and game shows often provide them with opportunities to practice listening to repetitive language. They can also use the newspaper, starting with captions for photographs, which provide a context and a limited amount of text.

Studying Individually

One of the most important things a teacher can do is provide students with the tools they need to work independently. For example, we can help them expand their vocabulary by showing them how to create a personal dictionary, use an English dictionary, and use context clues to decode meaning.

> *Mary*: Unfortunately, some English words have so many meanings that dealing with them out of context is hopeless. I remember a student who pored over a dictionary to find out what "having an affair" meant. The dictionary gave six definitions for "affair," including "a romance." This was not much help. In fact, the context clues in the text were much more useful, once she found out how to use them.

Conclusion

When the students contribute to selecting the content and process, it fosters a sense of power and comradeship with the teacher and the other students. When they feel they are listened to, their confidence increases.

By clarifying expectations and helping students understand the rationale for and intended outcomes of activities, teachers play a critical role in ensuring that students are able to learn effectively. Well-planned, well-organized activities help them feel that they are using their time well and that they are respected.

· · · · · · · · · · · · · · ·

BECOMING

A DYNAMIC TEACHER

When we reach the stage where the insights and skills talked about so far in this book have become second nature and we're at ease with the processes involved in teaching, it's time to move on the next phase. To become dynamic teachers, we need to continue to learn and grow throughout our careers—to renew ourselves professionally.

While juggling the immediate demands of the classroom is enough for beginning teachers to cope with, teaching involves much more than this. We need to consider our responsibilities and the roles we can play beyond the classroom. For example, we may wish to become active in our place of work to help improve the services offered to learners. We may also wish to contribute to the development of the ESL field or play an advocacy role with respect to ESL issues in our communities.

Developing Professionally

Our initial training is only a first step on the path to becoming a dynamic teacher. It is essential that we continue to learn throughout our careers; we are never "finished" teachers.

Rather than relying on experts to prescribe how things ought to be done, we must consider and try out new ideas ourselves. As teachers, we are the experts at the classroom level. We know the students—and their needs and goals. We know our own teaching style. When we're attracted to new ideas, we test them to ensure that they suit the students in our classes and that they work in the real world.

Reflective teaching is grounded in the classroom. We are constantly engaged in examining what we do and what happens in our classes, thinking critically about our attitudes and approaches. As we evaluate and improve our skills, we must be ready to consider making changes in the way we teach.

We can learn a lot by reflecting on our daily experiences in the classroom, especially if we invite students to give us feedback by asking questions like, "What did you learn today?" "What did you learn when we did X?" and "What do you need more practice in?" This also encourages students to think about and take responsibility for their own learning.

As we gain confidence, we become ready to involve the learners at a broader level. In addition to inviting them to comment on the content and process of specific lessons, we can encourage them to become partners in the reflective process, which involves gathering data, identifying and analyzing problems, proposing and testing solutions, and evaluating the outcomes.

Gathering Data

Any problem-solving effort starts with the gathering of data. As a session progresses, we act as careful observers, noting what works and what doesn't, as well as the unmet needs revealed in classroom activities and through students' questions. As we become better acquainted with the students, we become aware of their personalities, talents and emerging goals. We also gain insights into the dynamics of the classroom—the students' interactions with one another and with us—and how these affect learning. For example, we may find that the students direct all communication to the teacher, never to one another.

When reflecting, it's often helpful to focus on specific aspects of the classroom process by asking ourselves questions such as the following:

— *Planning*: Do the goals reflect the result of the needs assessment? Is the plan so sparse that I feel unprepared? Is the lesson plan cluttered with detail and difficult to follow?

— *Implementation*: What is the relationship between the plan and what actually happens in the class? What happens to cause changes in the plan when the class is in progress? Does the plan tend to be either too long or too short? How is the pacing?

— *Classroom management*: Do groups work effectively? Why are some students not participating? Are some students inattentive?
— *Talk*: Do students understand explanations and directions? Am I talking too much? Do students have enough opportunities to practice speaking and listening?
— *Evaluation*: Do students know what they have accomplished? Do I know what they have accomplished? How am I evaluating the lessons?

To gather data, we note our observations during lessons and take five minutes after class to review and add to these. Recording our notes in a journal works well because insights often come to us as we are writing. In *Reflective Teaching in Second Language Classrooms* (see "Additional Reading"), Jack Richards and Charles Lockhart suggest reflective questions to guide the writing of journal entries.

In addition, we can make audio or videotapes of the class to view later, elicit feedback from the students, or ask another teacher to observe the class and provide feedback.

Our own observations are, of course, subjective. Tapes are more objective, but they take time to review. For this reason, taping a particular activity, such as a brainstorming session, is a good starting point. If colleagues are invited to observe, orient them to the lesson and ask them to observe a particular feature. Of course, it must be understood that their observations are confidential. Students should also be reassured that the purpose of the visit is not to evaluate them.

Identifying and Analyzing Problems

Once observations are gathered, it's time to put them to use. Do they reveal problems? Which problems can we do something about? While we can't change the students' personalities, we can change the classroom process and our reactions to the dynamics of the class.

Problems come in layers; the issue that presents itself initially may, in fact, be merely a symptom of a deeper problem that is likely to become clear as we gather and analyze data.

For example, if students are reluctant to participate, the real problem may lie in one or more of the following areas:

— *Talk*: The teacher talks too much. Students don't understand instructions. Teacher's questions don't stimulate discussion.
— *Attitudes*: The students are not used to participating. Students expect teacher-dominated lessons.
— *Tasks*: Tasks do not encourage students to become actively involved. Tasks are too demanding. Tasks don't meet students' needs.
— *Skills*: Learners don't possess the skills needed to participate fully. Students need more—or less—practice.

Supportive colleagues can often help us analyze data. When we share our concerns with peers and with students, we gain partners in learning.

Finding Solutions and Taking Action

When searching for solutions, we must think things through thoroughly and be careful not to jump the gun. Are we dealing with the real problem, not the symptom? Part of this process involves considering possible outcomes. How we can alter the situation by changing our behavior?

Once a course of action is selected, give it a reasonable try. Don't reject it because it didn't work the first time. This often requires persistence and, sometimes, adaptations must be made. It's important to let the students know what we're trying to do and encourage them to comment.

Evaluation

The final stage in the process involves evaluating the changes we've made. Have they resolved the problem? While our own observations are important, it's also worth asking the students for their comments on how well the changes worked. Problem-solving is a cyclical process. As we work our way through it, other issues inevitably crop up. Through a cycle of reflection, action and further reflection, we strengthen our teaching skills and help the students learn.

One of the great satisfactions of teaching is that it is a "growth occupation"; we never stop learning.

Informal professional development occurs as we reflect on our teaching and discuss issues with colleagues over coffee or lunch, read journals and newsletters, and peruse publishers' displays at conferences. We can also learn more about teaching by participating in program initiatives, such as curriculum development, sponsored by the institutions we work for.

Formal professional development opportunities are offered by workshops, conferences and courses for ESL teachers sponsored by professional associations. Furthermore, universities and colleges often provide learning opportunities. When we engage in professional development, however, we need to cast a critical eye over the work of presenters and speakers and on published texts and materials. Ultimately, we need to become researchers, analyzing and testing ideas ourselves.

As we gain experience, it's often helpful to specialize in particular areas, such as developing listening skills or designing group tasks, or to focus on helping students with particular needs. Developing expertise in a particular area is satisfying and means we have more to share with colleagues.

Functioning in an Institutional Context

While our primary responsibility as teachers is, of course, to the students, we are also responsible to the institution in which we teach. We must work harmoniously with all our colleagues—students, other teachers and administrators.

One of the joys of teaching is working with supportive colleagues, whether this is through team-teaching, sharing ideas, developing curriculum, or working with teachers in other programs to help ESL students cope. By providing mutual support, we can help one another generate ideas, work through problems, and develop a sense of collegiality.

In most settings, teachers are accountable to the administration of both the ESL program and the institution as a whole. To show that we're meeting students' needs, we may be required to keep attendance records and report on both students' progress and the content covered in class. We may also be expected to participate in assessing and placing students, selecting materials, developing curriculum, evaluating courses and programs, and professional development activities.

Keep in mind that it's also up to us to act as advocates for the ESL students within the institution. Because of the language barrier, ESL learners are often less well-equipped to get the ear of administration than mainstream students. A variety of strategies can help ensure that their needs are made known:

— Invite administrators to visit the class.
— Invite administrators to staff meetings to discuss issues affecting learners and the ESL program.
— Keep administrators informed about the changing character and needs of the ESL students.
— Identify resources needed in the ESL program and make these known at budget time.
— Make efforts to work cooperatively with professionals and students in other programs.
— Write reports and make presentations to suggest ways of addressing unmet needs.
— Be aware of outside funding opportunities and suggest ways of tapping into them.

Functioning outside the Institution

Our concern about the ESL field may mean cooperating with other institutions that offer ESL programs, participating in professional groups, and working with volunteers.

Institutions often cooperate in ways that involve teachers. For example, we may participate in the articulation process, in which programs are compared so that students who move to another institution can be appropriately placed. Institutions may also offer professional development activities for one another.

We can also participate in professional organizations, which operate at local, regional and national levels to improve services for ESL learners, provide professional development opportunities for teachers, and deal with ESL issues at a political and professional level. Involvement in these groups gives us a broader picture of ESL programs and teaching opportunities and helps us stay up-to-date on developments and research in the field.

Working with volunteers is also important. Although volunteers provide invaluable services, there is no doubt that they add to the teacher's workload. They need training, support and materials, and their work must be monitored. As volunteers come to understand the needs of ESL students, however, they can become advocates for the program.

ESL programs are an educational and social response to immigration policy and the needs of minority language groups such as the Francophones in Canada and Spanish-speaking people in the United States. Educational institutions design and deliver these programs, as do many cultural and social agencies, government departments, funding bodies and citizenship services. These organizations need to work together to find ways of effectively serving the learners. For example, by talking to counselors in cultural agencies, we can get a better picture of the needs of students and, possibly, feedback on our programs. At the same time, we can keep agencies informed about educational opportunities for their clients. In the process, we gain additional insights into how we can strengthen our role as advocates for ESL students—and help students become advocates for themselves.

Conclusion

Teaching is a demanding field, and teaching ESL to adults is especially so. We must be ready to operate on many levels at once, balancing the many needs students bring to class. We must be knowledgeable about language, culture, citizenship and community, skilled in planning and facilitating learning activities, and flexible in adjusting them as circumstances change. We also need excellent interpersonal skills.

Although our first responsibility is to teach effectively, we can also help the students by contributing to activities and organizations that support the provision of ESL programs. We can also help by keeping community organizations and the public informed about their value.

As we teach, we continue to learn. We learn about language, language-learning, language-teaching, students and, of course, ourselves.

. . . .

ADDITIONAL READING

√⁺ Azar, B.S. *Fundamentals of English Grammar*. Englewood Cliffs, N.J.: Prentice Hall/Regents, 1992.

Bell, J. *Teaching Multilevel Classes in ESL*. Toronto: Pippin Publishing, 1988.

Brindley, G. "The Role of Needs Analysis in Adult ESL Programme Design." In *The Second Language Curriculum* (R.K. Johnson, Ed.). Cambridge: Cambridge University Press, 1989.

Brookfield, S.D. *Understanding and Facilitating Adult Learning*. San Francisco: Jossey-Bass, 1986.

⁕ Celce-Murcia, M. (Ed.). *Teaching English as a Second or Foreign Language*. (2nd ed.). Boston: Heinle & Heinle, 1991.

Gilbert, J.B. "Pronunciation and Listening Comprehension." In *Current Perspectives on Pronunciation: Practices Anchored in Theory* (J. Morley, Ed.). Washington, D.C.: TESOL, 1987.

⁕ Gilbert, J.B. *Clear Speech: Pronunciation and Listening Comprehension in North American English*. (2nd ed.). New York: Cambridge University Press, 1993.

Graham, C. *Jazz Chants*. New York: Oxford University Press, 1978.

Gunderson, L. *ESL Literacy Instruction: A Guide to Theory and Practice*. Englewood Cliffs, N.J.: Prentice Hall/Regents, 1991.

Helmer, S. & C. Eddy. *Look at Me When I Talk to You: ESL Learners in Non-ESL Classrooms*. Toronto: Pippin Publishing, 1996.

Klassen, C. & J. Robinson. *An Approach to ESL Literacy Assessment.* New Westminster, B. C.: Ministry of Advanced Education, Training and Technology, 1992.

Larsen-Freeman, D. *Grammar Dimensions.* Boston: Heinle & Heinle, 1994.

Law, B. & M. Eckes. *The More Than Just Surviving Handbook: ESL for Every Classroom Teacher.* Winnipeg: Peguis Publishers, 1990.

Mendelsohn, D. "Making the Speaking Class a Real Learning Experience: The Keys to Spoken English." In *TESL Canada Journal,* Vol. 10, No. 1: 1992.

Nilsen, D.L.F. & A.P. Nilsen. *Pronunciation Contrasts.* New York: Regents, 1971.

Nunan, D. *Understanding Language Classrooms: A Guide for Teacher Initiated Action.* New York: Prentice Hall, 1989.

Nunan, D. *Designing Tasks for the Communicative Classroom.* Cambridge: Cambridge University Press, 1989.

Nunan, D. *Language Teaching Methodology: A Textbook for Teachers.* New York: Prentice Hall, 1991.

Nunan, D. & J. Burton. *Beginning Reading and Writing, Oral Proficiency: Survival to Social.* Sydney: National Centre for English Language Teaching and Research, Macquarie University, 1989.

Oxford, R. *Language Learning Strategies.* New York: Newbury House, 1990.

Prator, C.H. & B.W. Robinett. *Manual of American English Pronunciation.* New York: Holt, Rinehart & Winston, 1985.

Richards, J. & C. Lockhart. *Reflective Teaching in Second Language Classrooms.* Cambridge: Cambridge University Press, 1994.

Wells, G. *The Meaning Makers: Children Learning Language and Using Language to Learn.* Portsmouth, N.H.: Heinemann, 1987.

Wrigley, H.S. & G.J.A. Guth. *Bringing Literacy to Life: Issues and Options in Adult ESL Literacy.* San Mateo, Calif.: Aquire International, 1992.

Wright, T. *Roles of Teachers and Learners.* Oxford: Oxford University Press, 1987.